Constance Frederica Gordon Cumming

The Inventor of the Numeral-Type for China

Constance Frederica Gordon Cumming

The Inventor of the Numeral-Type for China

ISBN/EAN: 9783337165758

Printed in Europe, USA, Canada, Australia, Japan

Cover: Foto ©ninafisch / pixelio.de

More available books at **www.hansebooks.com**

Photo by Ovinius Davis, Edinburgh.

THE REV. W. H. MURRAY.

The Inventor

OF

The Numeral-Type
For China

BY THE USE OF WHICH

ILLITERATE CHINESE
BOTH BLIND AND SIGHTED

CAN VERY QUICKLY

BE TAUGHT TO READ AND WRITE FLUENTLY

BY

C. F. GORDON-CUMMING

AUTHOR OF "WANDERINGS IN CHINA," "AT HOME IN FIJI," "FIRE FOUNTAINS
OF HAWAII," ETC. (PUBLISHED BY BLACKWOOD)
"TWO HAPPY YEARS IN CEYLON," ETC. (PUBLISHED BY CHATTO AND WINDUS)

DOWNEY & CO. LTD.
12 YORK STREET, COVENT GARDEN, LONDON
1898

CONTENTS.

	PAGE
A Brief Explanation	1-8
Biography and first sixteen years in China, working as Colporteur and for the Blind	9-88
Numeral Type adapted to the Sighted	89-121
Letters from Competent Witnesses	122-132
The Lord's Prayer in Four Types	134, 135
Explanation, with Illustrations, by Professor Russell, of the Imperial University of Peking . . .	133-144
Members of Committee, and Finance	155-158
Index	159-161

LIST OF ILLUSTRATIONS.

	PAGE
Photo of the Rev. W. H. Murray	*Frontispiece*
Braille's Embossed Symbols	22
A page from Murray's Primer	25
Blind Chinaman led by Boy	31
Blind Peter and his Bride	42
The Rev. W. H. and Mrs. Murray	53
Ch'ang, the Blind Apostle of Manchuria	80
The Numeral Type for Blind and Sighted	90
A page of Numeral Type	93
Musical Notes in Numeral Type	97
The Rev. W. H. Murray's Four Eldest Children	109
Plan of Peking	115
The Lord's Prayer in Four Types	134, 135
Tables of all the Symbols used in Numeral Type	137-144
Table of Mnemonic Sounds	146
Braille's Raised Dots	148
Symbols in Numeral Type	149
Tones (how indicated)	150
Reading Lesson	152

INTRODUCTION.

A BRIEF EXPLANATION OF THE SYSTEM.

A SIGHTED Chinaman learning to read his own book must be able to recognize at sight AT LEAST FOUR THOUSAND COMPLICATED CHARACTERS.

It was, however, pointed out by Dr. Morrison, the first Missionary to China, that (as is stated in the native dictionaries) there are only about FOUR HUNDRED AND EIGHT DISTINCT SOUNDS IN MANDARIN-CHINESE, WHICH IS THE LANGUAGE OF FOUR-FIFTHS OF THE WHOLE EMPIRE. Therefore, when Mr. Murray longed to teach the blind, he aimed at finding some method by which to represent four hundred and eight sounds.

Of the various methods hitherto invented in Europe for teaching the blind, none expresses fine gradations of sound so clearly as the system of embossed dots evolved by Mr. Braille. By taking a group of six dots, and omitting one or more at a time, SIXTY-THREE SYMBOLS CAN BE PRODUCED. These Mr. Braille arranged as representing the twenty-six letters of our alphabet, and various syllables, also musical notes.

But as the Chinese have no alphabet, and it is necessary to represent four hundred and eight sounds, MR. MURRAY SOLVED THE DIFFICULTY BY MAKING THE EMBOSSED DOTS REPRESENT NUMERALS; the same group of dots, differently placed, representing units, tens, and hundreds.

Ten groups represent units, 1, 2, 3, 4, 5, 6, 7, 8, 9, 0.

Any two of these symbols placed together represent tens, e.g. 4 0 = 40.

Any three represent hundreds, e.g. 4 0 8 = 408.

HE THEN NUMBERED THE FOUR HUNDRED AND EIGHT SOUNDS OF MANDARIN CHINESE, as spoken at Peking. Thus No. 1 stands for A; No. 2 represents Ang; No. 12 suggests Chang; No. 108, Hsiang; No. 123, Jan; No. 181, Liang; No. 302, Shuang; No. 393, Ying, and so on (as anyone can see for himself in Professor Russell's most clear explanation of the system; see Table A in the Appendix).

The pupils having learnt this list by heart (which they do with remarkable facility), thenceforth find that the touch of the dots representing any numeral, instinctively suggests the corresponding sound (just in the same way as to us the merest glance at certain letters of the alphabet suggests certain sounds, e.g. we do not spell PLOUGH or ROUGH, we utter the words without a moment's hesitation, although the letters represent such different sounds).

On an average the blind pupils learn to read and write fluently in less than three months from the date of their first lesson. Many have done so in half that time.

For ten years (i.e. till 1889) Mr. Murray's invention was supposed to be only for the blind. Then he realized its infinitely wider application, namely, FOR THE USE OF ILLITERATE SIGHTED PERSONS, who would never have time or patience to learn to read their own complicated ideographs. HE FOUND THAT he had only to adapt the Numeral Type for their use BY THE VERY SIMPLE METHOD OF USING BLACK LINES, PLAINLY VISIBLE TO THE EYE, INSTEAD OF THE RAISED DOTS EMBOSSED FOR THE FINGERS OF THE BLIND.

The result surpasses his highest expectations. IN LESS THAN THREE MONTHS the most ignorant peasants, instructed by blind teachers from books prepared for sighted persons by the pupils in his School for the Blind, find that they can read more fluently than the average Chinaman can do after several years' study of the Chinese ideograph. MOREOVER, THEY ACQUIRE SIMULTANEOUSLY THE ART OF WRITING CORRECTLY, which in the ordinary Chinese method is a separate study, and so very difficult that comparatively few persons ever master it.

The value of this invention in all Mission work is evident, when it is considered that throughout China almost all Christian converts are illiterate persons, who would never attempt to acquire their own bewilderingly intricate hieroglyphics, and who can only be taught by ear, and even that, perhaps, only on very rare occasions. Now those who take the very small amount of time and trouble necessary to master this system, can take any book printed in Numeral Type to their own homes, and read to themselves and their neighbours. So each convert will become a far more effective home-missionary than heretofore.

A most interesting point in this invention is that if Murray had intentionally set himself to try to invent some easy method for the use of illiterate sighted persons, he would almost inevitably have devised something alphabetic, with curved forms—both abhorrent to the Chinese, as being essentially "foreign." Whereas the great merit of this Numeral Type in their eyes lies in the fact that THE REPRODUCTION IN BLACK LINES OF BRAILLE'S SYMBOLS, AS PRIMARILY ARRANGED FOR THE FINGERS OF THE BLIND, NECESSARILY PRODUCES SQUARE OR ANGULAR FORMS, which appear to them to be a wondrously modified and simplified form of the square ideograph which they so deeply revere. Moreover, IT CAN EASILY BE WRITTEN IN COLUMNS WITH THE TINY BRUSH AND INDIAN (OR RATHER "CHINA") INK TO WHICH THEY ARE ACCUSTOMED, and its crowning merit is that the Chinese all HAVE A NATURAL LIKING FOR NUMERALS. So on all these grounds the new type rather appeals to their admiration, as does also the VERY SIMPLE AND EFFECTIVE ADAPTATION OF NUMBERS TO SHORTHAND for both blind and sighted writers.

The objects of the Mission may be briefly summarized as follows:—

    I. WORK FOR THE BLIND.

    II. WORK BY THE BLIND FOR THE BLIND.

    III. WORK BY THE BLIND FOR ILLITERATE SIGHTED PERSONS.

AN EXTEMPORIZED MAP OF CHINA.

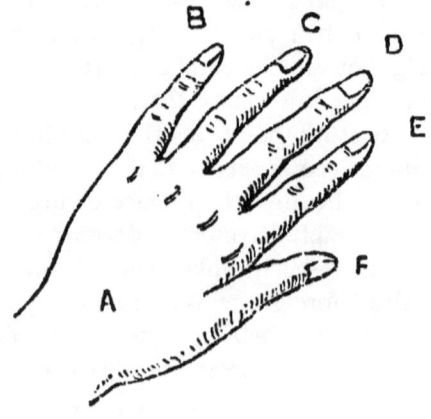

Look at the back of your left hand.

The four fingers, from A to B C D E, represent the Provinces in which Mandarin Chinese is spoken, and for which Mr. Murray has adapted his Numeral Type. (See NOTE on page 132.)

The thumb, A to F, represents all the non-Mandarin districts in the South-East, and very varied dialects to which it has NOT been adapted.

THE
INVENTOR OF THE NUMERAL TYPE FOR CHINA.

"The people that sat in darkness have seen a Great Light."
"They bring a Blind man unto HIM."

"It is always interesting to trace the genesis of any important cause,—to note the small beginning out of which momentous results grow. How much more so, when the issues at stake are for Eternity, and when development and advance mean the growth of the Kingdom of Righteousness."—MRS. DUNCAN MCLAREN.

AMONG the innumerable inventions of the present day, there is one so simple, and produced by a worker so humble, that it is in danger of being overlooked; and yet so vast are its latent capabilities, that I have no doubt whatever that it is destined to prove a most valuable handmaid to all missionary effort in China. It is already available for all those Provinces where Mandarin-Chinese is spoken, that is to say, in four-fifths of that vast Empire, and it is quite possible that its simplicity and cheapness of production may eventually lead to its being adapted to the varied non-Mandarin dialects which make up the remaining fifth.* These are the dialects spoken at

* As regards the various dialects spoken in China, there are no greater authorities than Dr. Edkins and Mr. P. G. von Möllendorff. In a paper read by the latter in December, 1894, before the China Branch of the Royal Asiatic Society (Dr. Edkins in the chair), he estimates that the Mandarin dialect is spoken by four-fifths of the inhabitants of China Proper. He reckons 300 millions who speak Mandarin, and 84 millions (chiefly along the coast of South and Central China) who talk other dialects, such as those of Canton, Amoy, Foochow, Ningpo, Shanghai and elsewhere, each of which is composed of a different number of sounds.

Shanghai, Ningpo, Foochow, Amoy, Swatow and Canton, which are all non-Mandarin, and are so very different from one another that each requires a separate version of the Bible, which has been printed for their use in the Roman alphabet.

It is only in non-Mandarin districts that this has been done, so that if Mr. Murray's confident assurance proves correct, and his invention is really shown to be capable of proving a blessing to four-fifths of the illiterate inhabitants of China, it must be admitted that the field open to him is a pretty large one ; and surely all who desire to spread the knowledge of the Gospel in that vast land, may well, not merely wish him success, but also do what in them lies to further his very uphill work.

The work of the Rev. W. H. Murray has only just come to the surface sufficiently to claim public recognition. Hitherto the little acorn which he has planted has been quietly germinating in the heart of the Chinese capital, known only to a handful of poor blind men and women, and scarcely even recognized by many of the little group of foreign residents in that city; and though there is every prospect that it will assuredly develop into a wide-spreading Tree of Life and Knowledge, destined to overshadow the whole land with its beneficent influence, it is as yet but a feeble sapling, whose growth, humanly speaking, depends on the fostering care of the Christian public.

Only those who have attempted to master the excruciating difficulties of any of the numerous dialects of Chinese, or the terrible array of intricate written characters which the weary eye must transfer to memory ere it is possible to read the simplest book, can fully appreciate the boon which has been conferred on the legion of the Blind in China, and now also on the illiterate Sighted, by means of the patient ingenuity of a Scotch working-man.

The calling to Mission work of the benefactor who has been enabled in so wonderful a sense to open the eyes of the blind, reminds me of one of the Bible stories, of how often, when GOD selected men for special work, HE summoned them from the plough, from the care of their flocks, from their fishing, mending their nets, or tent-making. And ONE WHO was LORD of all, consecrated all honest work, by choosing to receive HIS early human training in the carpenter's shop.

William H. Murray (who was born at Port Dundas, near Glasgow, on June 3rd, 1843 *—the only son in a family of ten children) would, in the natural course of events, have adopted his father's profession as a saw-miller, but for an accident by which, when about nine years of age, while too fearlessly examining the machinery, he lost his left arm, and was thus disabled—an apparent calamity which was the first link in that chain of events leading up to a discovery which, if properly developed, may prove an incalculable boon to millions yet unborn in the Celestial Empire.

So rude a check to his love of machinery doubtless led to greater diligence in his school studies, and so soon as the lad was able to work for his living, he obtained employment as a rural letter-carrier in the neighbourhood of Glasgow. In this, however, the subject of Sunday work proved a serious difficulty, which he solved by giving up two shillings a week of his scanty wages in order to be freed from an obligation against which his conscience revolted. His sacrifice, however, bore good fruit, for the earnest remonstrances of this young postman proved the commencement of that widespread movement which has secured so large a measure of Sabbatical rest for his comrades in the service of the Post Office.

His own longing was to obtain employment in some form of Mission work, and again and again he applied to the

---

* Mr. Murray's family lived at St. George's-in-the-Fields, St. George's Road, Glasgow. He believes the date of his birth to have been June 3rd, 1843, but is not positive as to the year, the first pages of the family Bible on which were inscribed these domestic entries having been accidentally burnt.

National Bible Society of Scotland. But though greatly attracted by the lad, the Secretary feared that one so unassuming, and apparently so very simple, would fail to prove a successful Colporteur, and, having given up the secure services of the Post Office, might be thrown, literally single-handed, on the world.

But, as the same Secretary now says, "What could he do against a man who was praying himself into the service of the Society?" For (though he knew nothing of this at that time) the young postman confided to him later, how he divided his long daily walk into three parts, and as he tramped along the monotonous road he beguiled a third of the distance by the study of the Holy Scriptures in the original Hebrew; the second beat was devoted to the Greek Testament;* while the last section was reserved for daily prayer that GOD would make it plain whether it was His purpose to employ him in direct missionary work, and whether from carrying Queen Victoria's Royal Mail, he might be promoted to become one of the Messengers of the GREAT KING in carrying HIS glad tidings to some far-distant heathen land.

At last, when in 1863 he renewed his application to the National Bible Society, his services were accepted, and he was commissioned to commence work among the ships congregated on the Clyde, and very soon the Society discovered that "it had never had such a Colporteur" as the gentle being who made his way among the sailors of all nations, readily acquiring such scraps of divers tongues as enabled him to effect more sales of the Holy Scriptures in foreign languages than had been accomplished by any of his predecessors. And yet (like another who, more than three thousand years ago, was called from the care

---

* His faithful friend, Dr. T. Brown Henderson, writes: "Murray and I studied 'Stokes on Memory' together. He used to pigeon-hole two hundred Greek words in an evening, and next day could recall them all quite easily, by his mnemonics."

of his father-in-law's flock to accomplish a great work) in his own mother tongue he is "not eloquent, but slow of speech."

This work amongst sailors was reserved for the winter months. In summer he was sent round wild districts in the Scotch Highlands, pushing his Bible-cart along many a lonely track of bleak moorland,—a task which, on hilly roads, must often have needed all the strength of this willing but only one-armed colporteur, who all the time was longing to be employed in carrying the Word of Life to those to whom it was yet unknown.

I wonder whether in those years of probation, he often found encouragement in the thought of how only a hundred years ago, William Marsham, bookseller's apprentice, sat down wearily in Westminster Abbey, grieving at the prospect of spending his life in carrying heavy book parcels, while Carey, the Baptist cobbler, was being snubbed by the assembled ministers for presuming to suggest the duty of commencing Foreign Missions! Yet notwithstanding all the drawbacks of general inertia, and the fewness of the workers, look at the results to-day of the work begun jointly by the bookseller's apprentice and the poor cobbler! Truly, in the spiritual kingdom, weak things of the earth are chosen to confound the mighty!

Perhaps Murray remembered how seventy years ago Morrison began Mission work in China, alone and despised, having to wait fourteen years ere he baptized his first convert. To-day, 100,000 in that great Empire own allegiance to his MASTER, and of these about 20,000 are habitual communicants in connection with one or other of the Protestant Missions.

Doubtless too, Murray's thoughts sometimes pictured the two humble Wesleyan missionaries, Messrs. Cargill and Cross, who in 1835 landed on one of the Fijian Isles, at the imminent hazard of their lives, yet resolved at all risk to carry the Light of Christianity to those ferociously bloodthirsty cannibals.* To-day, not alone in the 200 isles of that fair archipelago, but throughout the beautiful groups which stud the South Pacific, not a trace of old heathenism remains.

Or his thoughts may have travelled to Livingstone, the Glasgow cotton-piecer, and to scores of other humble human agents, and from one and all he would gather the same lesson of earnest care in doing the very best for the work now committed to each one of us—no matter how trivial it may seem, assured that it must be the best preparation for whatever else we may be destined to accomplish.

Ere long, Murray's remarkable aptitude for languages attracted the notice of some of the Directors of his Society. It was suggested that he might attend classes at the Old College in the High Street (a friend helping him to pay his fees), provided his studies nowise interfered with his regular work. All day long, therefore, through the gloomy Glasgow winters he stood in the streets beside his Bible waggon, hurrying back to his lodgings for a hasty supper; then studying till 9 o'clock, and rising daily at 3 a.m. on the chill wintry mornings in order to prepare for his classes at College from 8 till 10 a.m., at which hour he began a new day's work of street bookselling.

At length his seven years' apprenticeship as a home colporteur were fulfilled, and in 1871 he obtained his heart's desire, and sailed for China, where it was arranged that he should remain six months at Chefoo, engaged in the bewildering task of learning to recognize at sight the 4000 intricate ideographs or written characters by which the Chinese language is represented on paper—characters which someone has aptly compared to the marks that might be left by a drunken fly that had dipped its feet in ink.

Of these, between 30,000 and 40,000 are to be found in

* See "At Home in Fiji," page 65, by C. F. Gordon-Cumming, published by Blackwood.

the Chinese dictionaries, and a very large number of these must be mastered ere the student can read the classics of Confucius. But for a very simple book such as the Bible, it suffices to have a thorough knowledge of 4000. We, who had only to learn twenty-six letters of the alphabet, can quite understand that the vast majority of the Chinese never attempt to learn to read, still less would they dream of learning to write.

The same aptitude for mastering crabbed symbols which had facilitated Mr. Murray's study of Greek and Hebrew, enabled this diligent student to acquire about 2000 Chinese characters in four months, when he started on his first pioneer journey to visit a city about 250 miles in the interior of the Province of Shang-tu. He invented a rude litter slung between four mules, as the most convenient method of carrying his books, and thus made his way safely along precipitous mountain roads, facing bitter cold, and many difficulties, but sustained through all discouragements by occasional gleams of great promise.

But it is not my purpose to enlarge on Mr. Murray's many and varied experiences during a quarter of a century of incessant work as a colporteur in various provinces of China, as also on his more adventurous expeditions into Manchuria and Mongolia, though these are full of stirring human interest, by no means lacking in quaint incident. Imagine travelling all day by difficult paths, crossing dangerous rivers, and facing all manner of perils, to find oneself at night glad to seek shelter in a wretched so-called inn, which proves to be little better than a miserable shed, wherein mules and men seek shelter together from the pitiless storm, where the scanty food is of the coarsest and most repellent to the foreign palate, and where the traveller, blinded by the dense smoke which pervades the house, is perhaps guided to the only "reserved" sleeping berth—the post of honour—which proves to be the coffin which the host is carefully cherishing for his own eventual use—the filial and most acceptable gift of his dutiful sons!

As regards work, Mr. Murray has sometimes had to face the discouragement and danger of waiting till riotous and antagonistic mobs grew weary of their own discourtesy to the gentle foreign teacher.

On one occasion, after he had thus patiently endured weeks of annoyance without effecting a single sale, the fickle folk suddenly veered round, and clamoured for the foreign "Classics of Jesus;" so that he could scarcely produce copies fast enough, and when evening came he found he had sold 3000 books! After this the people in that city became so friendly that they would not hear of his leaving them, so he remained there for six months; his knowledge of machinery and of shipping details proving an unfailing source of interest to the crowds who thronged him; and it is almost needless to add that the influence thus acquired was invariably used as a means to edge in the subject which ever filled his heart.

Since his arrival in China he and his Chinese assistants have sold upwards of 260,000 copies and portions of the Holy Scriptures in the Chinese character. Many of these have been purchased at great fairs by merchants and influential men from remote districts, and some copies even found access within the sacred precincts of the jealously-guarded Imperial Palace many years before the Empress consented to accept the Book which was so specially prepared as her birthday gift. Truly, were this the sole result of Mr. Murray's accident, it would have proved no trifling gain to his fellow-men.

But interesting as are all efforts for imparting spiritual light to those into whose hearts it has not yet shined, the work which is so emphatically Mr. Murray's own peculiar Gift, is that of enlightening those who are also physically blind. One of the first things which deeply impressed him (as it must impress every traveller who looks around him in the densely crowded streets of Chinese cities) was the extraordinary number of blind men who mingle in every crowd, some going about alone, or guided by a child; others in gangs of eight or ten, each guided by the man in front of him, while the leader feels his way with a long stick—a most literal illustration of the blind leading the blind. A gentleman assured me that he had on one occasion seen no less than 600 miserable blind beggars all assembled to share a gratuitous distribution of rice!

This very large proportion of blindness is due to several causes, such as leprosy, small-pox, neglected ophthalmia, and general dirt, to which, in great tracts of North China, we must add the stifling dust and smoke caused by the lack of ordinary fuel, which leads the people, all through the long, parching summer, to cut every blade of sun-dried grass, and turf sods, to heat their ovens. This produces a dense smoke, which penetrates to every corner of the houses, causing the eyes to smart most painfully.

Now when you consider the size of the vast Chinese Empire as compared with our little England (which is barely the size of the smallest of the Eighteen Provinces, and not a third of the size of the larger ones), and recollect that in our favoured land, where the ravages of small-pox and ophthalmia are so effectually kept in check, there are nearly 40,000 blind persons, to say nothing of the multitudes whose sight is seriously defective, and when you come to think that, although there is only provision for about 3000 in asylums, yet it is very exceptional to see even one blind person in England, you can readily understand that when we roughly estimate the blind of China at 500,000 (that is to say, an average of one in 600, supposing the population not to exceed 300,000,000), we are probably very far below the mark.

Many of these blind men and women are simply most miserable beggars, hungry and almost naked, lying on the dusty highway and clamouring for alms, or else yelling frightful songs in most discordant chorus, to an accompaniment of clanging cymbals, beating small gongs or clacking wooden clappers, producing such a din that the deafened bystanders gladly pay the infinitesimal coin which induces them to move on. A considerable number earn their living as fortune-tellers, and play dismally on flutes to attract attention. These men carry a board with movable pieces something like draughts, each marked by a symbol, by means of which they pretend to foretell lucky days, and answer all manner of questions. Thus for unnumbered centuries have the blind legions of China dragged through their darkened, dreary lives, a burden to themselves and to all around them, and as to the possibility of teaching them any useful way of earning their living, that seems never to have occurred to any Native philanthropist.

And yet blindness seems to be the only form of human suffering for which the average Chinaman feels a certain moderate degree of pity. Few are so utterly debased as to rob a sightless man, and such are generally addressed by a title of respect, as Hsien-Shêng, i.e. Teacher, although the adult blind are, as a class, about the most disreputable members of the community—so bad that even a hopeful soul like their friend Mr. Murray is compelled to admit that the majority appear incorrigible.

All his hopes, therefore, rest on training young lads, and so far as possible isolating them from their seniors, for whom he fears that comparatively little can be done. But by taking boys in hand as early as possible—some as young as seven years of age—he has good hope that (as spotless paper may be evolved from foulest rags) so from this, the worst class of the people, he may rescue many, who, under careful training, may not only attain undreamt-of gladness for themselves, but may also be made the means of incalculable good to their fellow-countrymen—truly a bright star of hope now rising on their gloomy horizon.

Of course, in this sweeping classification of the adult

blind, there is room for many bright exceptions, and, indeed, the first thing which attracted Mr. Murray's attention to the present work was the fact that amongst the crowds who (with true Chinese reverence for all written characters) pressed forward to purchase the copies or portions of Holy Scripture which he offered for sale at a very cheap rate, blind men sometimes came, likewise desiring to purchase the "Classics of Jesus," as our Bible is called by men accustomed from their infancy to reverence "the Classics of Confucius." When he asked why they wanted a book which they could not see to read, they replied that they would keep it, and that perhaps friends who could read would sometimes let them hear it. Then he would tell them how, in Europe, the blind are taught to read and even to write; but this they never could believe, for he seemed to them as one that mocked, so utterly incredible did it appear that any one should learn to read with his fingers.

But the more he saw, the more grievous did it appear that absolutely nothing was done for those darkened lives by any Christian Agency known in Peking, and he began to plead their cause amongst the missionaries of various nations, whom he could reach. These, however, very naturally replied, "We Christian missionaries of all Protestant denominations put together, are in the proportion of one to one million of the population. How can we undertake any additional work? Perhaps in the next generation, if there are ten times as many missionaries, and ten times the funds now available, something may be done for the Blind of China."

Still, as he went about his daily task, mingling with ever-changing crowds, in scorching summer and freezing winter, this thought was never absent from his mind. Failing to awaken human sympathy, his soul was the more ceaselessly absorbed in prayer that some means might be revealed to him whereby he might help these poor neglected sufferers.

He had need of truly GOD-given patience, for eight years elapsed ere he arrived at a satisfactory solution.

The first step in the right direction was when he realized that although at least 4000 complicated characters are used in printing even a simple book, there are really only 408 distinct sounds in Mandarin Chinese, which is the language of about 300,000,000 of the people. Something to this effect is stated in the native dictionaries, which led Sir Thomas Wade to prepare a Peking syllabary of 420 sounds. These, however, Murray found it possible to reduce to 408. So he aimed at representing 408 symbols.

Ere leaving Scotland he had mastered Professor Melville Bell's system of Visible Speech for the instruction of the deaf (which he found so greatly facilitated his own study of the very difficult language, that he has prepared a pamphlet on the subject, for the use of all foreign students). It occurred to him that this might be adapted to the use of the blind, his first idea being to reduce all Chinese sounds to symbolic forms. He went so far as to have these made in clay and baked, so that they could be handled. From these some blind pupils learnt to read; amongst others who were thus taught was a deaf mute. But this system was cumbersome and unsatisfactory—all the more so, as it occurred to the teacher that as the Chinese adore their own written hieroglyphic characters, they would probably render Divine honour to these clay symbols!

Moreover, during his residence in Glasgow, his interest had been so deeply aroused by seeing blind persons reading by means of Moon's system of embossed alphabetic symbols, that he had set himself to master it. Now he ceaselessly revolved in his own mind whether it might be possible to adapt it to the bewildering intricacies of the non-alphabetic Chinese language, with all its perplexing Tones," which by almost inappreciable difference of pronunciation, cause one word to convey a dozen different meanings. But he very soon realized that this system, which cannot represent musical notes, could never be satisfactorily adapted to the amazingly fine gradations of sound which prove so maddening to the foreigner who is learning Chinese.

It was not till long afterwards that he learnt that twenty years previously Dr. Moon had produced portions of Scripture in his own type in various Chinese dialects, by which some blind persons in the Southern Provinces had been taught to read.

The solution of the problem was brought home to Mr. Murray in a very simple and touching manner. In the London Medical Mission where he lodged, a little daughter of the house, Mina Dudgeon, had been born blind, and for her use books were sent from Britain in Braille's system of embossed dots—a system which expresses fine gradations of sound so clearly, that the most complicated music can thus be written for the blind. By taking a group of six dots, arranged in two rows of three, so as to form an oblong, and omitting one or more at a time, sixty-three symbols can be produced. By means of these, we of the Western World, represent the twenty-six letters of the alphabet, which so accurately express the forty-one sounds of the English language, and the balance of the sixty-three are left to denote punctuation and musical notes.

But the Chinese have no alphabet, and it was necessary to represent at least 408 sounds. How could Braille's sixty-three symbols be made to do this?

After long perplexity, and many months devoted to experiments, there was vouchsafed to this patient seeker after his LORD's guiding, a Vision which he recognized as a distinct Revelation,—a belief which surely no Christian will be inclined to gainsay. In the broad noonday, while resting from his long morning of exhausting toil (bookselling in the street under the blazing sun, among noisy Chinese crowds), suddenly, as clearly as he now sees one of his stereotyped books, he seemed to see outspread a great scroll, whereon was embossed in Braille's dots, the whole system which he has since then so patiently and ingeniously worked out. Then the thought seemed to be flashed into his mind, "MAKE THESE DOTS REPRESENT NUMERALS, AND

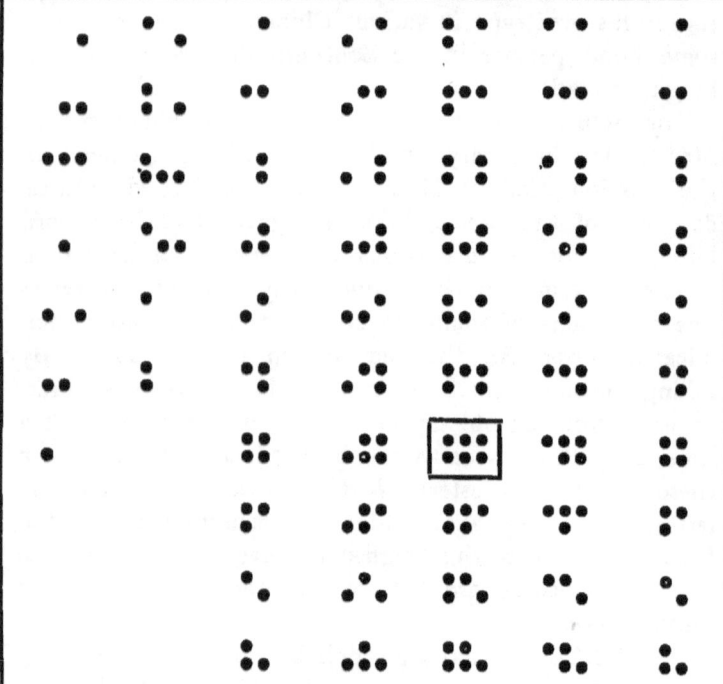

Table to show how six dots can be varied so as to produce the sixty-three groups by means of which Braille represents letters and music.

THEN NUMBER THE SOUNDS." * There, in a nutshell, lies the whole secret.

* It is interesting to learn that when (a good many years after Murray had perfected his system) the telegraph was introduced into China, the only practicable system was found to be that of numbering the 6000 characters most commonly used, and telegraphing the number only. Thus the precise characters are indicated with smallest possible risk of any confusion. This, of course, involves a knowledge of the Chinese ideograph.

It must not be inferred that Mr. Murray's Vision at once brought him "to the desired haven" in regard to its practical application. But the Inspiration thus received was as a chart by which he was enabled carefully to work his way through a thousand perplexities—a labour of love to which he devoted every hour that he could steal from sleep or rest, through eight long years. For deeming himself bound to devote every moment of the day to direct work for the Bible Society, it was only after "business hours" that he allowed himself to work out the details of this, his special interest.

I have already explained in the Introduction how HE DECIDED TO REPRESENT EACH OF THE TEN NUMERALS, 1, 2, 3, 4, 5, 6, 7, 8, 9, 0, BY ONE OF BRAILLE'S SYMBOLS; BY COMBINING THESE, ALL OTHER NUMBERS ARE OBTAINED. For instance, it is clear that to represent the number 387, it is only necessary to place the symbols 3, 8, and 7 one after another. When the deft finger-tips are passed over the symbols 3, 8 and 7 in immediate succession, the ready mind instantly suggests the number 387, and by the law of association which, natural and unerring in the mind of the blind, takes the place of sight, the sentence in the Primer beginning 387 and closing with the sound *yâng*, springs into mental vision, and the pupil involuntarily utters the sound *yâng*.

SIMILARLY THE ENTIRE 408 NUMBERS CAN BE REPRESENTED BY THESE TEN SYMBOLS. BUT FOR THE SAKE OF DISTINGUISHING EACH WORD FROM THE PRECEDING, FIVE INITIAL SYMBOLS ARE ADDED, used solely to represent the first numerals of the five groups of numerals between 1 and 99, 100 and 199, 200 and 299, 300 and 399, 400 and 408, respectively, so that when the finger-tips rest upon any one of these five initial symbols, the pupil discerns the beginning of a new word.

With this equipment of 408 sentences, and fifteen of Braille's symbols, the pupil is ready either to read or write Chinese Mandarin Colloquial without the tones.

If both tones and sounds are to be indicated, then fifteen more symbols are employed, making thirty in all, and leaving thirty-three symbols to indicate punctuation and musical notes.

A very important feature is that no symbol is ever employed for more than one purpose. Hence there is no confusion in the mind of the pupil arising from the use of the same symbol, sometimes as a mere initial, and at others as an entire word.

Having thus apportioned the thirty symbols, Mr. Murray proceeded to write the numerals 1 to 408, marking beneath each, one of the 408 sounds, and as an aid to memory, he arranged 408 doggerel lines connecting each numeral with its corresponding sound, as children say,—

   One—to make ready.
   Two—to prepare,
   Three—to be off,
   Four—to be there.

Of course for grave Chinamen who only reverence the wisdom of Confucius, Mr. Murray has to arrange suggestive sentences, such as No. 7, which stands for K'u, or bitter, so the line is, " Bitter lips are a disgrace," &c.

These are printed on four sheets, and divided into groups of five lines each.

The pupil has in the first place to be taught these by heart, and as all the Chinese are endowed with singularly retentive memories, they find no difficulty whatever in doing so very rapidly, and thenceforth THE MOMENT THE FINGER TOUCHES ANY NUMERAL, the mind instinctively flashes over the line, and RECOGNIZES THE FINAL SYLLABLE AS THE SOUND REPRESENTED, AND *vice versâ* FOR WRITING, GIVEN A SOUND, INSTANTANEOUSLY ITS NUMBER IS NAMED.

What could be conceived more simple? And it has proved so in practice, for from that day to this, THE MOST IGNORANT BLIND PERSON WHO HAS TAKEN THE TROUBLE TO TRY TO LEARN HAS ACQUIRED THE ARTS BOTH OF READING

| 150 | 149 | 148 | 12 | 11 | 10 | 9 | 8 | 7 |

一百五十弟離似乎遠些來到我家也不犯作客

一百四十九弟兒北邊住的就是你哥哥

一百四十八弟兒費許多的工夫為甚麼刨坑

十二替你還這筆錢你更該我的賬

十一弟打兒是因為要分家產

十弟撕破了的書總得用糨糊粘

九北山上有好些樵夫打柴

八非是念經就是吃齋

七給你錢不是叫你喝酒是叫你喝茶

A page from Murray's Primer, giving a sample of the four thousand Chinese symbols, and their simple equivalent in embossed dots, which in no case exceed three groups, representing units, tens, and hundreds.

AND WRITING FLUENTLY IN LESS THAN THREE MONTHS. AND NOW SIGHTED PERSONS ARE LEARNING BY EXACTLY THE SAME SYSTEM. In point of fact many persons, both blind and sighted, have mastered the system in half that time, whereas the average Chinaman takes several years to acquire the art of reading his own Chinese books in a very hesitating manner; the very difficult art of writing being a totally separate study and so difficult that only a comparatively small number even attempt to learn. Of course many bright students, who can give a good deal of time to the study of the Ideograph, do learn to read in a much shorter time, but I am assured that six years is the average. This is a most important point, for in Murray's simple system the pupil acquires simultaneously the power of reading and writing, and the latter is so rapid that a good pupil writes on an average twenty-two words per minute.

Great was Mr. Murray's joy when he had so far arranged his system that he could make it understood by those for whose good he had so long toiled. He determined first to try whether it could be acquired by a poor old blind man, "Mr. Wang," who was crippled with rheumatism, and like to die of want. He provided the old man with such creature comforts as ensured a quiet mind, and then with the aid of a native colporteur commenced teaching him, and soon, to the unspeakable joy of both pupil and teacher, the poor rheumatic fingers learned to discriminate the dots, and the blind man was able to read the Holy Word for himself.

Just then a blind man, Mr. Lee, "a tall, handsome man, aged forty-two," was brought to the medical mission, having been severely kicked by a mule which he had inadvertently approached, his long guiding stick passing between its legs. This man was induced to beguile the hours of suffering by the study of the new system. He proved an apt pupil, and within two months could read well, though his finger-tips were roughened by age and work.

The next pupil was a poor lad who had become blind,

and who, having no one to provide for him, had been left to starve, and, when quite helpless, had literally been thrown on to a dung-heap and there left to die alone. He was found by a man who had known his father, and said he was a good man, and that it was a pity to leave the lad to perish ; so having heard of the foreign bookseller's extraordinary care for the blind, he actually resolved to risk the expense of hiring a cart, and brought the poor starving boy to Mr. Murray's lodgings, begging him to try and save him. Three months of careful nursing, with good food and needful drugs, restored him to health, and he soon was overjoyed by finding himself able to acquire the honoured arts of reading and writing.*

Mr. Murray next selected a poor little orphan blind beggar, named Sheng, "a little thing scarcely human in appearance," whom he often observed lying naked in the streets in the bitter cold of winter, but who, notwithstanding his loneliness and poverty, always seemed cheerful and content, and who, moreover, had the special recommendation of being free from all taint of leprosy (an important consideration when you are bringing a guest to stay in your house). He took this lad in hand, washed and clothed him, and undertook to feed and lodge him, provided he would apply himself in earnest to mastering this new learning. Naturally, the boy was delighted, and we can imagine his ecstasy, and the thankful gladness of his teacher, when *within six weeks* he was able, not only to read fluently, but to write with remarkable accuracy—better, indeed, than many sighted Chinamen can do after studying the ordinary method for upwards of twenty years!

It was at this stage, in June, 1879, that I first made acquaint-

---

* So very practical is the honour accorded to learning that a literary man is exempt from all the varieties of most ignominious corporal punishment which figure so largely in Chinese Courts of Justice (or rather, of Injustice!). A scholar in presence of the magistrate simply bows, and stands erect, whereas a merchant or shopkeeper must lie prostrate, with his head on the ground before the great man.

ance with Mr. Murray and these four pupils, the very first rescued from the dreary darkness of blind life in North China.

I had been travelling for about twelve years—years of pleasant, aimless drifting, with no special object beyond that of filling large portfolios of water-colour sketches, and seeing as much as possible of the manners and customs of far-distant countries. After some interesting months in Southern China, I decided that I had had enough of wandering in foreign lands, and so resolved to return home.

I had actually secured my ticket from Shanghai to San Francisco, when various friends urged me not to leave China without visiting Peking, the great northern capital. To do this involved a long and expensive journey, and I had really no wish to see anything more. But it seemed as if I HAD TO GO, for my friends were persistent, and at the last moment the kind consul came to tell me that a pleasant English family had just arrived on their return journey to Peking, and that they would undertake all the trouble of securing my boat for the three days' journey from Tientsin up the Peiho river, and engaging carts for myself and luggage at the end of the journey. So all was made so easy for me that I had to give in, cancel my steamboat ticket to San Francisco, and secure one to Tientsin instead.

My many kind friends in Shanghai had all (in truly Eastern fashion) decided that I must be the guest of certain foreign residents in Peking, to whom they despatched introductory letters. Had their intention been carried out, what I now believe to have been the reason why I was led to Peking at that time, would have failed, for I should certainly have seen nothing of Mr. Murray or his work. But the Guiding, in which I so firmly believe, as directing all the smallest details of our lives, had caused a missionary lady at Tientsin to have occasion to send a special messenger to the London Medical Mission at Peking, and in her letter she mentioned that she had just been helping to furnish my boat with the necessary comforts for the three days' slow journey up the Peiho.* That letter bore good fruit, for on my arrival, I was met by a messenger bringing me the most cordial letter of welcome from Dr. and Mrs. Dudgeon, of the London Mission, bidding me consider their house my home for as long as I wished to stay in Peking. So that day found me comfortably established in a Chinese bungalow beside the London Mission Hospital, where all day long Dr. Dudgeon was ministering to sick and suffering Chinese patients.

Lodging within that same compound was Mr. Murray, the colporteur of the National Bible Society, and (as all my busy friends had to divide the troublesome task of escorting the traveller with an insatiable thirst for sightseeing, to all the chief points of interest in the great capital), my gentle countryman took charge of me when, in the small hours of the morning (from 3 to 5 a.m.), he went to try and sell books to the retainers of the Tartar nobles, on their way to or from the Imperial Palace, when attending the Emperor's early levees.

Thus we became excellent friends, but it was not till some days had elapsed that he summoned up courage very shyly to ask if I would come and hear his blind men reading. Of course I did so, but without in the least realizing how great had been the difficulties to be overcome, or how different was the system to those which have so long made blind readers familiar objects in our own streets.

All the same, it struck me as intensely pathetic, as we stood at the door of a dark room—for it was evening, but that made no difference to these blind readers—to hear what I knew to be words of Holy Scripture, read by men who, less than four months previously, had sat begging in the streets in misery and rags, on the verge of starvation, now full of delight in their newly acquired power, truly salvage from the slums of Peking. Thus it was that by

* See "Wanderings in China," by Miss C. F. Gordon-Cumming, vol. ii., page 136. (Published by Blackwood.)

what we are wont to call "the merest chance," I became an eye and ear witness of these first samples of Mr. Murray's teaching.

It might naturally be supposed that on my return to Britain I at once endeavoured to awaken practical interest in this new effort to bring Light and Gladness to so numerous a class of sorely afflicted fellow-creatures. But this was not the case. It did not at the moment impress me much more than if I had seen a very small school for the blind in Europe, and (engrossed as I was with the innumerable and very novel scenes to be visited in China, and in my subsequent travels in Japan and the Sandwich Isles) it seemed for a while to have passed from my remembrance.

Then followed my return to Scotland, and the engrossing interest of writing those records of my wanderings,[*] which have secured to me so many friends personally unknown, many of whom have in later years helped very practically in the development of this work.

It is still more remarkable that no one else seemed then to realize what a wonderful Baby-Giant Murray had evolved, and so for eight years more he continued to work on almost unknown even to his few countrymen in Peking, scrupulously throwing all his energies into street-preaching and book-selling in all recognized working hours, and only devoting the time he could strictly call his own, to elaborating the details of his system, and training as many pupils as he could feed and teach. This, of course, meant sacrificing the noonday rest (so essential to one whose work often began about 3 a.m.), and stealing hours from the night, often after long days of hard travel, exposed to scorching sun or freezing wintry blasts.

So the development of the work was hindered both by lack of time and of funds, being limited to what could be accomplished by the willing and continual self-denial of the working-man, to whose patient ingenuity the whole exist-

[*] See Catalogue on last page.

William Simpson, F.R.G.S.

BLIND CHINAMAN LED BY BOY.

ence of the system is due. And assuredly it must have taxed his slender salary to the very utmost to provide board, lodging and clothing for his indigent blind students, and make the modest sum intended to keep one man, feed and clothe several. For when one poor helpless lad after another seemed thrown upon his hands, he felt that it was impossible to reject those so manifestly entrusted to his care, and of course he could not leave them to earn their living as street beggars while he was trying to teach them.

Very touching is the first account of this beginning of work as described by Mr. Murray, when writing in May, 1879, to his friend Mr. W. H. Slowan—Western Secretary of the National Bible Society—specially interesting, as telling of "the new-born rill" which has now developed into a gently flowing rivulet, and is assuredly destined to become a broad river of Water of Life.

He describes his very first pupils, and how he had (naturally) hesitated ere undertaking another. "Then I thought if I could only take care of the odd pennies I might have him for a pupil too. After some thought and prayer, I asked him to join Ting in his studies, so now Ting calls for him and they come along together. We can hear the rattle of their long sticks some time before they appear, like husband and wife, arm in arm! It is half-past nine in the evening. The three *ku-sao*—blind ones—are busy at their work. Just now I have been over to see what was going on. I could see nothing till I returned for my lamp. Sheng (so recently a naked little street beggar) is sitting as happy as a king between the two men, each with a table of his own. . . . These three could now easily teach other six, but I have gone as far as my means allow, as each must have for his support (i.e. for actual food) about thirteen shillings a month. If I could only get six churches, each to maintain one blind man, we could have a school of nine, the blind teaching the blind."

This letter and appeal were inserted by Mr. Slowan in

the "Quarterly Record" of the National Bible Society for October, 1879, with a special reference to "the self-denying and generous efforts of one whom the Society is honoured to have as its representative at Peking." He pointed out what heavy expense Mr. Murray had already incurred for this benevolent effort, and added, "There should be little difficulty in finding half-a-dozen congregations willing to give £10 each for a year's training and support of so many blind Chinamen, who will, it is hoped, in their turn, help to diffuse the knowledge thus gained." He somewhat unfortunately added a footnote to say that Mr. Thomas Coats, of Paisley, who had long been personally interested in Mr. Murray, had generously placed £100 at his disposal for this purpose—I say unfortunately, because it seems to have been assumed that no further help was required, so that appeal in the "Quarterly" does not seem to have brought any responses.

Very quietly, but very steadily, Murray worked on from 1879, when he had perfected his system, till 1886, training his little band in the humble schoolroom which he himself had hired, and in which they not only studied but lived, as, in order to isolate them from grossly contaminating surroundings, he found it necessary to feed, clothe, and lodge them.

After awhile he earnestly appealed to the National Bible Society of Scotland to undertake the moderate expense of enabling him and his blind men to print the Scriptures for the use of such blind persons as could be induced to learn to read.

This was refused, as it was considered that the invention was still at an experimental stage. (Yet Samson and Solomon were once infants!) Thus Mr. Murray was left to find money for the project where he best could.

In April, 1883, Mr. S. Dyer, agent at Shanghai for the British and Foreign Bible Society, visited Peking and was much struck by the work done in Mr. Murray's Blind

School. "Some of the boys wrote something to dictation. Others were called in and read it off to them; then played a tune on the harmonium." Mr. Murray asked "whether the British and Foreign Bible Society would help him in bringing out the Scriptures in the Numeral Type for the Blind?"

This request was forwarded to the Rev. William Wright, D.D., who, thinking it strange that an agent of the National Bible Society should have to seek aid from another Society in carrying out "what seems to be an admirable system for teaching the Blind to read the Scriptures," wrote to the senior Secretary, the Rev. W. H. Goold, D.D., to ascertain his views on the subject. Dr. Goold replied in August, 1883, that his Committee were not disposed to take up this work for the blind, but that they would rejoice should the British and Foreign Bible Society see their way to do so.

So the British and Foreign Society supplied the necessary materials for producing the first edition of St. Mark's Gospel and the Acts of the Apostles, embossed by the Blind themselves at the little school in Peking, specimens of these being sent to London as soon as they were prepared. Consequently to this Society belongs the credit of having been the first to recognize and officially aid the infant Giant.

Encouraged by this beginning, Mr. Murray, in November, 1883, again applied to the National Bible Society of Scotland to ask if they would not authorize the publication of the Book of Genesis and the Gospel of St. Matthew? His friend, Mr. Slowan (the Western Secretary), who had been in South Africa at the time of his previous application, was now at headquarters, and was able to send him the sanction of the Committee to produce these books, provided the cost did not exceed £20. He added, "I hope you will always find us ready to do all we can for one of our best men."

So since then a succession of small grants for materials have been made by the National Bible Society, which have enabled Mr. Murray and his blind men, working in their own school, to produce all the principal books of the Bible for the use of the Blind. Then when the infinitely wider application of the Numeral Type, as adapted for the use of Sighted persons, more especially THE ILLITERATE POOR, had been fully proved (by the pupils themselves printing small editions of the four Gospels, and several Epistles, besides hymns and reading lessons) the N.B.S. in 1893—1894 yielded to Mr. Murray's importunity so far as to authorize him to print FOR THE SOCIETY an edition of 2000 copies of St. Mark's Gospel, with notes—a small first step towards what will, we believe, prove a very great development of the Society's work in China.

But I must return to the early days of the Blind School. Besides perfecting the details of his system of reading and writing, and making experiments in teaching his pupils various industrial arts, he very soon determined to give them some training in music. And here I may note how wonderfully some men and women contrive to make the very most of very small advantages in the way of teaching, while others are mere sinks of learning, which never reappears in any form for the good of others.

The only musical teaching Mr. Murray had ever received was a sufficient knowledge of the Tonic Sol Fa system, to enable him to teach the scholars at a Sunday-school, in which he taught at the time when he was a postman in Glasgow. All else he has evolved for himself.

In the first place he thought it would be a help to possess some musical instruments, so on several occasions when foreign residents were leaving Peking, and their very dilapidated pianos or harmoniums were sold for a few dollars, he bought the apparently worthless old things, and (although he has only one arm) he contrived, with the help of one of his Chinese assistants, to supply new wires, reeds, or leathers—whatever was lacking—and made them once more give forth musical tones, and on these he has taught several of his blind pupils to play so well, that they are now the organists of various Mission Churches.

It is a remarkable fact that the blind seem almost invariably to be endowed with a marked faculty for music, and though, when left to themselves, they naturally indulge in the horrible caterwauling which passes for music in the Celestial Empire, they very easily acquire European tunes, and not only pick up a new air very rapidly, but remember it accurately—a very important qualification for all engaged in pioneer Mission-work, in which the value of singing, as the handmaid of preaching, is being more and more fully recognized in all parts of the world.*

Now here is another marked advantage of Mr. Murray's ingenious adaptation of Braille's system. So marvellously does it lend itself to the representation of sound, that all musical notes and terms in the study of harmony have for many years been thus rendered in Europe and America, where a considerable musical literature has therein been prepared for the blind of all nations.

So early as 1881, music was recognized as an essential part of the training in the humble school at Peking, the blind students writing out musical scores from dictation with wonderful accuracy, as part of their regular morning lesson. (To the uninitiated the symbols representing musical notes look exactly the same as those representing

---

* So fully is this the case in regard to America's Foreign Missions, that the New England Conservatory of Music at Boston now invites all who are studying for Mission-work to accept its teaching *free of charge*, that they may not only have the opportunity of studying Church and chorus music, and sight-singing, and may be instructed in piano and reed-organ tuning, but may also acquire such a knowledge of the fundamental principles of harmony, as may enable them to arrange native music, and write the accompanying parts ;—in short, that they may be taught *how to teach others* both vocally and instrumentally. This musical training is now offered, because experience has proved that *much of the deadness and apathy in many Missions has been due to its neglect*, whereas the most successful Missions have invariably been those in which singing was largely employed.

ordinary sounds, and we could not tell a page of music from a page of any book.)

Their writing-frames and paper being adjusted, all wait with style in hand, ready to begin, and in about twenty minutes they produce a perfect score, perhaps one of Sankey's hymns in four parts. Then, with great pleasure to themselves, they pick out the tunes on the piano, harmonium, or American organ,—beginners being taught by having the embossed symbol pasted on to each note ; so then each student reads the written score with one hand, while with the other he finds out the notes.

Having thus mastered the tunes, the blind organist and choir sing their Christian lyrics in the chapel, which is open to all comers ; and when a good congregation has assembled, attracted by the music, one of the students addresses the people, and afterwards recommends those who can read to purchase a copy of the Holy Book, that they may study it for themselves. Thus, at the close of the day, the sales by the blind lad have sometimes proved to be larger than those of the Bible Society's authorized agent.

No wonder that to their countrymen it should appear little short of miraculous that blind beggars should be thus cared for by foreigners, and endowed with apparently supernatural powers—indeed, had it not been that Mr. Murray had so thoroughly won the confidence of the people by his constant intercourse with them while Bible-selling in the streets, they would assuredly have attributed the whole work to magic, and thus irreparable harm would have been done. As it was, many even of the adult Christians found it so incomprehensible that, for awhile, they deemed this reading with finger-tips to be accomplished by clever jugglery—a sort of sleight of hand.

Speaking of musical instruments, Mr. Murray gives some suggestive details of the difficulties of keeping these in repair, in a climate subject to such excessive heat and cold (to say nothing of their being subject to such incessant practising!). Finding that those in the school had become semi-dumb, he called in the aid of the invaluable Blind Peter, and a Chinese tinker, and took them to pieces, when he found reeds broken, sound-boards split, and bellows burst. With much ingenuity they contrived to repair these so thoroughly, that the instruments were again fit for use. When one thinks of three harmoniums and a piano all going simultaneously, in so confined a space (to say nothing of so many human voices, including those of young children, with occasional variations on banjo, guitar, dulcimer, and concertina), and that, in such summer heat as makes noise almost unendurable, one cannot but pity those whose lot is cast within earshot thereof!

On first realizing with what facility the Blind could acquire the power of reading, there seemed good reason to hope that a great multitude of miserable Blind beggars would be transformed into useful Scripture Readers, certain to attract great attention in the streets of Chinese cities, not only by the novelty of the thing, but because the man who is able to read is deemed worthy of much honour. This sanguine hope, however, was not entertained by those who knew the true character of those with whom they had to do, the adult blind in China being notorious for the grossest immorality; their night refuges in Peking bear so vile a character, that Murray himself has never ventured to visit them.

To teach such men and allow them to become street readers would be manifestly wrong, and would degrade the office of Scripture reader in the eyes of the Chinese. So, from the beginning, Mr. Murray has devoted his always limited means, to teaching only men of hopeful character, either already Christian, or likely to become so. And his chief hope lies in taking young lads, and keeping them till they are thoroughly trained. For, as he justly says, if in our own land, where all surroundings are at least influenced by Christianity, we deem it necessary to train our future teachers, first at school, then at college, till a strongly Christian character is formed, how much more is this necessary in a land where every child is from its earliest infancy trained in idolatry, and steeped in all the gross habits of life and thought, inseparable from heathen surroundings.

So he has taken as many boys as possible, with excellent results.

Very touching is the story of most of these poor waifs. For instance, having resolved to adopt a blind lad who came to his door begging, Mr. Murray visited the wretched parents in their miserable home, where the father lay suffering tortures from rheumatic fever, and the only other child was also blind. Soon afterwards the father died, and the mother brought her second boy to commit him to the care of this good friend. But in giving her two sons the parting kiss, the poor bereaved creature sank to the ground in an agony of tears and lay prostrate, weeping bitterly for two hours; her grief appealing so intensely to the sympathy of the other blind lads and men, that all united in a chorus of sobs and tears. So deeply were the neighbours touched, that notwithstanding their own deep poverty, they raised a small subscription, to help her on her journey to a distant friend; the blind lads adding the few cash which they had received as presents.

One of the brightest lads, and the sweetest singer, was brought to the school by a man who had rescued him from a most horrible death; his cruel father, not caring to be troubled with a blind son, having thrown him into a foul pit of semi-liquid sheep's dung, and there left the poor little minstrel to suffocate. Happily he was rescued just in time, and his singing proved none the less joyous for that terrible experience. That was a most literal case of " salvage."

One of the earliest and most satisfactory pupils was one

known as Blind Peter. He was only twelve years of age when he was led to Mr. Murray's door by his elder brother, aged fourteen. They were on their first begging tour, and had travelled 150 miles from their native town, where both parents had died of fever. The elder brother, whose sight was good, said he could work, and earn enough to keep himself, but could not provide for two without having recourse to begging, from which he shrank ; so he entreated Mr. Murray to take charge of his brother, promising to return ere long, to ascertain whether he was found capable of learning. But, evidently fearing lest the blind lad should be returned to his care, the elder brother did not return for two years, by which time the bright little fellow had proved himself an eminently satisfactory scholar, the best hand at stereotyping, and most reliable in all departments of work ; having moreover so marked a talent for music, that he subsequently became organist in the Chapel of the London Mission. When the elder brother returned, Mr. Murray took him into the school, and without speaking a word placed his hand in that of the younger, who instantly recognized the touch ; the two stood speechless for a moment, then tears began to flow, and he retired, leaving the two together to talk over their varied experiences.

Of course there was no further question of Peter resuming his travels. It was plain that he was on his way to earn his own living by teaching others, and making himself useful in a thousand ways, and thenceforth this was his never-failing record. By degrees he rose to be Mr. Murray's right hand in all departments of the school, taking charge of all new pupils on their arrival, and teaching them most successfully. To quote Mr. Murray's own words : "Blind Peter, the young man of our own training, is now at the head of affairs in the school, and has proved the best teacher we could have, in pushing the boys forward. He drills them well, and is fully qualified to advance them in all the branches, especially in music, vocal and instrumental. He is quite a musical genius, and has written out and learnt by heart all our hymns. He is now the regular organist of the London Mission Chapel, and is invariably invited to play when he attends any Chinese meeting in the various English or American chapels. I have been advised to apply, on his behalf, for the post of organist to the Emperor, who has now got an organ for himself. But I think that he has nobler position where he is, and will do and get more good in teaching his blind countrymen."

Of course a blind organist has to know all his music by heart, and as an instance of the wonderfully retentive memory of the Chinese, which is especially remarkable in the blind, Mr. Murray mentions that at very short notice a new hymn-book was adopted by the London Mission. He and Peter set to work, arranged plans, found the new tunes, and Peter wrote them out embossed from dictation, and by the aid of Mr. Murray's system of memorizing, within two months he had mastered the whole book, so that as soon as a hymn was given out, he knew the appointed tune for it. As the book contains more than four hundred hymns, even a Chinaman could not have done this without the aid of the system of mnemonics.

Peter also became a very earnest and persuasive preacher.

When in May, 1890, Mr. Murray attended the great Missionary Conference held at Shanghai, he took with him Peter, as a most practical illustration of the results of his system of teaching the blind, and Peter's excellent reading, writing, and playing the church organ, won enthusiastic appreciation from that great assemblage gathered from all parts of China.

Naturally, on his return to Peking his fame went abroad, and doubtless tended to influence a very pleasant sighted girl, who having been brought up in a Christian school (the American Presbyterian), was allowed the unheard-of privilege of selecting her husband from half-a-dozen available young men. She unhesitatingly selected Peter, as being

BLIND PETER AND HIS BRIDE.

the best, cleverest, and best looking of the lot, stating her views in the most matter-of-fact terms to the woman who acts as professional go-between in arranging such family matters. So as her widowed mother and elder brother approved, the damsel allowed her hair to hang over her forehead in a fringe, which in China is the recognized sign of an engaged maiden, the marriage contract was drawn up on a sheet of lucky scarlet paper, and marriage settlements were arranged according to Chinese custom by Peter undertaking to make a regular allowance to his mother-in-law.

They seem to have been a very happy couple during their brief years of married life, although their home was saddened by the death of their three little ones.

Alas! in the autumn of 1895, while Mr. Murray and his family were in Scotland for a brief period, they received letters from Peter, telling of failing health. He was apparently a victim of the dread consumption which has proved fatal to so many of the most promising students. He wrote that he feared he would have passed away ere his dear friends returned to Peking, but happily he and they were spared that trial. They returned early in autumn in order to reach Peking ere the Peiho river was frozen, so Peter had the joy of welcoming them back, and handing over to their keeping all the interests left in his charge. It was not till the following spring that he was translated from his life-long physical darkness to the unspeakable joy of " beholding the King in His beauty," in the land where there is no need of the sun, because the Lamb Himself is the Light thereof.

In thus sketching the career of one of Mr. Murray's first pupils, I have gone far ahead of my main subject, which was the early stages of Mr. Murray's school, from its very beginning in 1879.

It was not to be supposed that all his pupils could turn out as satisfactory as Peter. Sad to say Sheng, the very first boy taught, whose prospects seemed so hopeful, was tempted just for one day to rejoin his former associates, that he might display his various attainments. He was decoyed away by a wandering blind minstrel, and though, after a while, he returned to his benefactor expressing much contrition, and was once more received into the school, he was found to have suffered such complete moral shipwreck, that for the sake of the others, his expulsion became necessary—a very bitter sorrow to the patient friend who had so rejoiced over his early promise.

Of course, tidings of the wonderful gift thus conferred on a chosen few, have brought others who, being able to maintain themselves, have come as self-supporting pupils. Thus one blind man arrived who had travelled 300 miles to put himself under Mr. Murray's tuition. Another came who was found to be endowed with talents which seemed so specially to fit him for the ministry, that he was transferred to an institution at Tien-Tsin where candidates are prepared for Holy Orders. There for about three years he studied under the Rev. Jonathan Lees, acting as organist to the Mission, and also going daily to the Hospital to read and speak to the heathen patients. Though blind, he was at the head of his classes, and was just finishing his training when his health broke down. Mr. and Mrs. Murray went to see him, and though he could hardly speak, he expressed so great a wish to return to his old home and friends in the Blind School at Peking, that arrangements were made for his return. But one fiercely cold night, with a wind blowing from Siberia, the spitting of blood returned, and could not be checked. Poor Wang was heard to pray that God would take him soon, for he was past work on earth. And God took him. He was much loved, and was so wise and good, that his death was a real loss.

Another Wang, a beggar-lad aged fourteen, showed considerable ability. "It was a pleasure to teach him," but alas! his constitution was already undermined by consumption, and he only lived long enough to give evidence of a new and enduring life begun—he died after he had been seven months under Mr. Murray's care. Everything that love could do was done for him, as indeed for all the pupils.

Another very encouraging pupil was a young man who lost his sight when he was about twenty. He rapidly acquired the blind system of reading and writing, and then set to work to stereotype an embossed Gospel of St. Matthew.

Mr. Murray has all along taught his pupils to do everything for themselves in the preparation of their books, even to the stereotyping, which by a very ingenious contrivance of his own invention, they are able to do so rapidly, and with such accuracy, that any one of these lads can with ease prepare considerably more work than three men in England will turn out in the same time, and will also do it more accurately, and at a far cheaper rate; and, of course, as long as such lads are students, they gratefully work for their keep. A London workman endowed with sight considers three pages of stereotyping to be a good day's work. A Chinese lad easily produces ten pages a day.

To quote Mr. Murray's own account of this :—

"It occurred to me that I could simplify the process of stereotyping, so instead of holding the punch in one hand, and having only the tip of the little finger to guide, while the other hand holds the mallet, I designed a table with a lever at one side, and a mallet to work by a treadle,—the mallet always to strike the centre of the table, and squared off the plane, over which the block would have to describe. The treadle is of course worked by foot, and with side woods, the width of two words, and woods the width of a double line, which exactly correspond in size with the latter; for the guide in shifting the block upwards in the plane of the fixed mallet, as the other, the side woods keep the position sideways; the stereotyper moves these as he finishes two words at a time, the top piece, at the finishing of the double line, is taken from the top, and pushing up the block, he puts that wood at the next foot, and then the block is in proper position for striking the next, and is firm and fast in its position.

"Thus, the right hand, which would otherwise have had to hold the mallet, is left free to handle the manuscript, and to relieve the tip of the little finger, and take to guiding. Now, with us the process is so simplified that the operator can work with great speed and pleasure.

"The advantage will appear best in the results, when I tell you that the boy can do with ease in one day what would take three men and one third in England to do in the same time. So what a sighted man would take twelve months to do, my blind boy will do in three months, and the quality of the work is struck more perfectly."

I think we could not have a better illustration of the wonderful laws of compensation, than this proof of the additional sensitiveness imparted to the finger-tips of the blind. Certainly amongst sighted persons, few of the most delicate hands possess so keen a sense of touch as to be able with closed eyes to follow even a line in primers prepared for English blind readers.

Among the many ingenious devices for the use of the blind, I may mention the envelopes in which their letters, embossed on large sheets of paper, travel so securely. When first pupils left the school to go to other districts as Scripture readers or in any other capacity, Mr. Murray feared they would get out of touch with him, as the most sensitive fingers could not read a letter in embossed dots, after it had been crushed in the common post. Then he happily bethought him of a pile of old tins in which sugar and oil had come, and calling in a Chinese tinker, he bade him cut these up and make a number of tubes, just large enough to hold a loosely-rolled sheet of paper. Now, whenever one blind man wishes to write to another or to

Mr. Murray, or to send off a new hymn tune, or anything else of special interest, he rolls up his letter, places it in one of these tin tubes, passing a string through to secure it. Then he pastes paper on the outside, which some sighted friend addresses, and away goes the letter by Chinese book-post—some of these, with their interpretation, have reached me safely in Scotland.

Thus, whereas it is an almost unheard-of thing for poor people in China to write to one another, the Blind trained by Mr. Murray can indulge freely in this solace at the smallest possible cost, and of course these cylinders can travel to and fro many times, so they are constantly carrying messages of counsel and love to former pupils, now widely scattered in distant parts of the Empire, and especially to the teachers of five Schools for the Blind, now commenced at Mission-stations in five different Provinces, who are thus kept in touch with the mother school at Peking, which indeed is to so many of them their only ideal of Home. Many, in writing back, dwell on this, saying that they always think of it as such, and of Mr. and Mrs. Murray as their true parents.

Mr. Murray's next invention (in 1880 to 1881) was one which bids fair to have a far-reaching influence for good, in that it will probably be received with enthusiasm by Chinese literary men, who are generally antagonistic to everything foreign. This is a system of SHORTHAND, so effective that those who have mastered it are able to produce a verbatim report of a whole sermon, and *it is so simple that the reporters have never the slightest difficulty in reading what they have written,* which is more than can always be said by shorthand writers in Europe!

He had himself learnt Pitman's system, and he wondered that a nation so literary as the Chinese, with their voluminous examination papers, should never have devised any such aid. Then it occurred to him TO ADAPT SHORTHAND SYMBOLS TO NUMERALS, and as he marks only the first and second element of each word, he has a distinct set of symbols for these, so as to avoid confusion.

Like the type which it represents, this Shorthand has as yet only been adapted to the use of those Provinces in which Mandarin Chinese is spoken, i.e. to four-fifths of the Empire. Naturally in so vast a territory the pronunciation varies greatly, but IN A SYSTEM WHICH IS EXPRESSED BY NUMBERS, NOT PHONETICALLY, this is found to be of no consequence.

His own account of it is as follows:—"In our shorthand style there are only two parts—initials and finals.* There are forty-one initials and ten finals; the latter are made up of two dashes, a hyphen and tiny circle given in four positions—upright, horizontal, slanting down to right, and the opposite. It is simple to learn, and allows considerable speed. Various contractions have been introduced, and a hundred words have been written in a minute in a neat hand. With constant practice a clever writer could easily double this number."

Not only is it rapidly and easily learnt, and written with speed and accuracy, but it is actually one of the lessons taught by the Blind to Sighted pupils! To enable them to do so, Mr. Murray invented a curious variety of the familiar "Black-board" of our schools. He got a joiner to cut out in wood ten complete sets of the Shorthand Symbols, each ten times the written size. One set of these he glued to a board 2 feet high by 5 inches wide. The carpenter also made three frames, each 10 inches by 5 inches, with a grooved line cut longwise, a little below the middle. The Blind pupils get a lesson from those glued on, and they then practise with the movable letters on the grooved board. They can thus show two words at a time, and they find it as interesting as a game.

---

* In case of any misunderstanding from the use of these terms, Mr. Murray explains that they do not refer to the principle, but TO THE FIRST ELEMENT AND SECOND ELEMENT, WHICH TOGETHER FORM EACH WORD.

When teaching Sighted persons the Blind teacher directs his pupils to copy these symbols one by one, till they can reproduce them accurately. Neither teachers nor learners seem to find any difficulty in this method, samples of which will be found on two of the Plates. (See pages 90 and 137.)

This shorthand is also applicable to writing music in two parts, treble and alto, which can be done at great speed.

The system is really so simple that Mr. Murray thinks intelligent students will have no difficulty in acquiring it by themselves. .. He has therefore now prepared a very careful explanation, with illustrations, which he got modelled and then sent to Shanghai to be stereotyped and printed on two cards, of a size to go in an ordinary envelope. He reckons their cost at about a penny per card, and intends to place them for sale in some of the shops which sell foreign goods (notably wine and spirits), and which are frequently visited by Chinese students, who, he believes, will certainly be attracted thereby, especially when a few have been helped by their use.

He mentions having just had a call from one of the eunuchs of the Imperial Palace, who is learning his Shorthand, and who brought with him a younger man, also one of the Palace eunuchs, who wished to see the School and to hear the boys read. So he lives in hope that influential men may ere long be interested in the work.

He is sometimes gladdened by hearing that his system has been adopted by foreigners for their own personal convenience, as in the case of Dr. Fryer of Shanghai, and the Rev. Dr. Corbett of the American Presbyterian Mission at Chefoo. He says:—"From time to time I receive evidence that our plans suit the wide field indicated, and that many we cannot enumerate, are using our methods. The actual number we can give, does not show the work that is going on, and which is sure to bear fruit by-and-by."

All this varied work was quietly carried on in the School year after year, receiving very small attention from even the foreign residents in Peking, and still less from any other folk.

It was not till 1885 (when I was writing my book, "Wanderings in China") that I realized in how great a measure it was still dependent on the small earnings of the inventor—a hard-working street bookseller—and then, for the first time, I understood that I had been constrained to make that journey to Peking (so entirely against my own inclination) in order that I might be able to tell the story of this earnest worker, and enable his countrymen and countrywomen to share the privilege of helping to develop his inventions.

So I then began writing about it to a multitude of newspapers and periodicals, and when my fiftieth birthday was approaching (May 26th, 1887), only two days after our Queen's birthday, I ventured to confide this fact to the many sympathetic readers of my books of travel, asking if any would gladden my own Jubilee by sending me such donations as would enable me to assist Mr. Murray in developing his wonderful inventions.

(I may add that I took special pleasure in thus utilizing my own grey hair as "a talent" to be devoted to the benefit of the only race who are so enlightened as to reverence all old women, simply BECAUSE THEY ARE OLD WOMEN!)

Then from all ends of the earth I received most kind responses, bringing me gifts for this purpose. Many of the letters were most pathetic in their references to blind friends and relations, or to those who had passed away—one mother sent a little packet of faded yellow paper containing a gold coin which had been the treasured fortune of her little son, long treasured by herself, and she felt that teaching a poor blind child was the most sacred purpose for which it could be used.

Little by little a sum of about £2000 was accumulated, and then I asked the National Bible Society of Scotland to administer this for Murray's special Work for the Blind. As the Society could not recognize that this was quite in its own line of business, several members of its Committee formed themselves into a separate Committee for this purpose. Thus it came to pass that in 1887 Mr. Murray's invention of the Numeral Type first obtained formal recognition as a definite and very valuable new factor in Chinese Mission work—work destined to bring a priceless blessing to all future generations of Blind Legions. For as yet we deemed it to be only "Work for the Blind," and we had no idea of its far wider and more important latent capabilities in relation to the illiterate Sighted. These were not discovered till three years later.

Meanwhile, Mr. Murray, being entitled to a year's furlough, had returned to Scotland, not to rest, as most of us would have done, but to work harder than ever! In the course of some of his Bible-selling expeditions in remote districts, he had on several occasions been visited by unmistakably genuine converts, who had become so, solely from reading the written Word, perhaps accompanied by some teaching from another convert. These have come to him asking for Christian baptism, although fully realizing all the persecution that would probably ensue.

It was most painful to have to explain to such earnest seekers that he was not qualified to bestow the Gift they desired, especially as it was more than probable that they might never again come in contact with any foreign missionary. Ere he left Scotland Mr. Murray was studying Divinity with a view to entering the ministry, but he had temporarily abandoned this intention when he was offered immediate work in China as a colporteur.

He now, therefore, resolved that on his return to Scotland he would ascertain whether any branch of the Christian Church could dispense with the usual lengthy course of Theological Training, and grant him Ordination after less than a year of special study. Finding that the United

Presbyterian College in Edinburgh might possibly do so, he entered himself as a Divinity Student, and absorbed himself in the close study of Theology, Greek, and Hebrew, as a pleasant relaxation from the Chinese dialects in which he had been steeped for the last sixteen years.

It is pleasant to learn that the merits of this earnest student were so fully recognized, that eminent representatives of the three Battalions of the Presbyterian Regiment took part in his Ordination, the venerable Dr. Andrew Bonar of the Free Church, and the Rev. Dr. T. Elder Cumming of the Established Church, having gladly accepted the invitation of the United Presbyterian Synod to assist in the service, which was held in Berkeley Street Church, Glasgow, on the evening of the 23rd June, 1887.

In Glasgow at about the same date, the Rev. William H. Murray found his bride, Miss Maggie Glen, whose devoted work among the very poor in the slums of that great city was good training for facing the manifold trials of life in the heart of a great Chinese city. Very soon after their marriage she accompanied him on his return to his loved work.

With part of the aforesaid "Jubilee Fund" a small property in Peking was purchased, on which stood old Chinese houses, one of which has until now been Mr. Murray's house, while the others were easily adapted to the use of the blind students, both male and female (of course in quite separate schools). A further sum was apportioned to the immediate expenses in maintenance and clothing of a limited number of pupils, rarely exceeding twenty at a time; while a portion was set apart as the very modest nest-egg for an Endowment Fund. This we deemed it desirable to secure, ere suggesting that Mr. Murray should resign his appointment as a colporteur, in order to have entire command of his time for the development of his special work, trusting to our raising the balance of his salary, as well as necessary funds for the maintenance of the school, by annual collections.

Photo by Ovinius Davis, Edinburgh.

THE REV. W. H. AND MRS. MURRAY.

But Mr. Murray knew the Chinese populace too well to risk the danger of falling out of constant touch with them. The work for the Blind was then still very new, and he said, " Were I to cease continually going about in the streets, and talking to the people, they would quickly forget me, and would soon raise a cry that my teaching of the blind was all witchcraft, and I myself a wizard, and perhaps some day they might come and pull down the school and maltreat all the inmates."

The street bookselling also helps to attract attention to the school. Thus we hear of a visit from one of the eunuchs of the Imperial Palace, who, observing the sale of Bibles in the street, found his way to the premises of the Blind Mission, where he bought a number of books and inspected the school. One of the pupils wrote to his dictation, and he carried off the paper, which may thus have received attention within the Palace.

So up to the present date—1897—Mr. Murray has continued to devote one-third of his time to colportage for the National Bible Society, while during the remaining two-thirds he is Principal of his own School for the Blind.

How well founded was his estimate of the danger of losing personal control of the ignorant superstitious mob was fully illustrated when, soon afterwards, two American lady doctors engaged Lu Tê (which is the Chinese equivalent of Ruth), one of the blind girls, who is endowed with a fine voice, to return with them to their hospital in another Province, in order to read and sing to the patients. This she did, to their great delight, and Mr. Murray was congratulating himself on the discovery of this field for usefulness for blind women, when the old, cruel superstition asserted itself, and the hospital was surrounded by an infuriated mob, who declared that now they had proof positive of all they had been told about foreigners bewitching Chinese men and women, and extracting their eyes to make medicine of them. It was evident, they said, that

Ruth had been so bewitched, and that her seeing to read with the tips of her fingers was all the result of witchcraft. They would certainly have wrecked the hospital had not poor Ruth, with much difficulty, been smuggled away, and restored to Mr. Murray's safe custody at Peking.

The commencement of a School for Blind Women was a very difficult matter. Of course, at first, only Mr. Murray and one or two of his earlier students were competent to teach. But these were all men or lads, and that a woman should be taught by a man is altogether shocking to Chinese notions of propriety. One blind woman, however, was resolved to learn, and allowed her relations no peace till they consented to interview Mr. Murray on the subject.

He suggested that a curtain might be hung, so that he could not possibly see the woman, but her hands might come through, and he could guide them when teaching her. This suggestion was actually under consideration, but was dismissed by the family conclave as being quite too improper. The difficulty was, however, solved when it was ascertained that one of the blind boys in the school was so young that he might be admitted within the women's quarters; so the blind woman secured him as her teacher, and every day this little chap came and taught her the lessons he had just learnt, and thus she acquired the arts of reading, writing, and of playing the concertina, and so she fitted herself to become the teacher of the few blind girls who, after Mr. Murray's marriage, ventured to come to the school thus strangely begun.

Amongst its earliest inmates were two little ones saved from untimely death. One poor little thing became blind from small-pox when she was only three years old. The woman who had adopted her as a daughter could not be troubled with a blind child, so resolved to poison her, when happily a foreign lady heard of the case and rescued the poor little creature, who soon became the pet of the school, and grew up to be a useful girl and a capital reader.

Another poor little waif was rapidly becoming blind, so her own parents decided to drown her, when happily the Murrays were able to save her, and she likewise became a good scholar.

The slow development of this female school has been somewhat disappointing, comparatively few women having as yet availed themselves of the privileges offered to them. As we all know, the greatest boons are not always eagerly accepted by those who need them most, and the Chinese notions of propriety as regards the seclusion of women are so strict that even poor peasants could not come to be taught in the same enclosure as the blind men. However, after the female school had been effectually separated from that for the men, a few Christian girls were sent from neighbouring Mission stations. One of the early pupils was "a kindly, simple-looking young widow, twenty-three years of age. The mother of one of our blind pupils saw her crying in the street, and was sorry for her, and came to tell us. We took her in, and she is doing well. She learnt to read and write in a few days. What a change of life! people at home cannot fathom it. But for the pupil's mother seeing her, what a risk she ran—a thousand to one against her."

A Manchu widow and her daughter, fifteen years of age, smart and promising, came about the same time; also an old widow from the London Mission, and a young girl from the Baptist Mission in another Province. Mi Chia, fourteen years of age, was sent by the American Mission at Peking, and Fri Pi, aged ten, came from a London Mission station two days' journey to the south of Peking. It was a striking testimony to the simplicity and effectiveness of Mr. Murray's system, that in six weeks, "these two bashful little girls mastered the Primer, and could read, spell, and write correctly," while, at the same time, they were learning Sunday-school lessons, and to sing hymns by heart.

Little by little, women hearing of such triumphs as these, are beginning to gain courage, and several Christian converts have come such long distances, and in the teeth of such difficulties and opposition as effectually shames our easy-going ways.

One of these arrived unexpectedly in the very depth of winter, when a bitter blast was blowing fiercely from the frozen plains of Mongolia. Mr. Murray was in the act of writing to me, describing the intense severity of the winter, when he looked up and saw a strange group in the court of the Blind School, namely, a coarsely dressed, toothless old Chinese peasant, leading a donkey, on which sat a poor woman, so muffled up to keep out the cold, that she appeared like a bale of goods. They had found the outer gate open, and had entered unchallenged. On being asked what he wanted, the old man mumbled out a reply totally incomprehensible either to Mr. Murray or his Chinese Bible-man (that is his native colporteur).

Twice the question was repeated with the same result, and the intruders were on the point of being turned out as ordinary beggars when the old man produced a packet containing two letters addressed to Mr. Murray, and from these he learned that the writer was a blind woman, twenty-seven years of age, wife of the old man, who was about sixty years of age. Their home is in Shantung Province, distant from Peking about 1400 li (equal to about 470 miles), and they had been twenty-five days on the journey, the woman sitting perched on one side of the quaint wheelbarrow, with only one large central wheel, which is the ordinary (and very uncomfortable) conveyance of the poor. The bundles of luggage are slung on the other side of the wheel, to balance the passenger. This was drawn and pushed by her husband and another man. In this difficult fashion, in a country practically without roads, they travelled till within a day's journey of Peking, when they exchanged the wheel-barrow for a donkey, in order to approach the capital in better style! The peculiarity of the Shantung dialect, combined with the loss of his teeth, accounted for the difficulty in understanding the old man's speech, which was as unlike ordinary Chinese as if it had been Russian.

Needless to say, the woman was quickly lifted from her donkey and taken into the Girls' School, where she was warmed and fed and comforted, while her husband, good old Chin Ma, was well cared for by Mr. Murray. It appears that the young wife is very intelligent, and has a happy talent for communicating to others whatever she herself acquires. So there seemed good hope that if she received a training at the Blind School, she might be able to commence work as a teacher in connection with the English Baptist Mission in Shantung. I think many persons who can see, would shrink from encountering all the dangers and difficulties of that long, long journey—well-nigh a month of incessant slow travel in the depth of winter; but "It's dogged as does it," and this undaunted couple determined to conquer all difficulties. So, leaving their two children in charge of a friend, they started on their toilsome way, sustained by a wonderful faith in all the good that may result from this hard pilgrimage to the capital, and from the teaching of the wise foreigner.

Is it not strange and touching to look back to the time when young Murray's arm was torn off in his father's sawmill in far-distant Scotland, and to remember that *that accident* was the first link in the chain of events which has thus opened a new world of good to these people, who have so long dwelt in darkness?

The young woman was, naturally, all impatience to begin her studies. Not being troubled with the distractions of sight, the mighty walls and towers and other wonders of Peking could not compete with the one thing she had come so far to seek, namely, the power of reading the Word of God; so it was arranged that after one day's rest her studies should commence, and then her good old man would start alone on his weary return journey.

Evidently her good example proved infectious, for in the following year another blind pupil arrived from the same mission. This was a girl fourteen years of age (or, according to Chinese reckoning, fifteen, as they count a child one year old at its birth). She also had made the long journey on the barrow with the one large central wheel, and had been wheeled all the way by her own father, who is a much respected and gifted native preacher—a man not accustomed to manual labour, and one to whom about twenty-five days of severe physical toil must indeed have been a serious undertaking. Well might Mr. Murray remark, "That is indeed the right sort of man to preach the Gospel of Love."

So different are the dialects of these two Provinces (although comparatively near), that when the girl addressed blind Mrs. T'sui, her future teacher, the latter was obliged to confess that she could not catch one word she said. YET BOTH LEARNT WITH EQUAL FACILITY, BOTH TO READ AND WRITE FROM THE SAME LESSON BOOKS IN MR. MURRAY'S NUMERAL TYPE.

I was telling this story at a meeting in Glasgow, when a card was handed to me, which proved to be that of Mr. Forsyth, the very missionary who had sent both these women to Peking. That was a pleasant corroboration on the spot.

Of the girls in school Mr. Murray said: "It is a picture for the heathen to see them going in a band every Sunday morning through the streets leading to the London Mission, where they always attend service. They look so clean, bright, and fair, their faces preaching the Gospel. What a contrast to the usual bands of blind singing girls!"

After a while he wrote about these: "The young girls are growing in stature and in grace. They are now about fifteen years of age, and are noble Christian little girls; only a fair opening is required to show how they would speak forth the Word of the Lord boldly. One of these was very bad, and we nearly despaired of her, she stole things, and concealed them so artfully, but that was long ago. She was then slovenly and idle. Now she is honest, bright, open-hearted, and does everything well. She has no home but the school, as her mother would sell her were she to return to her."

In China, even more than in other heathen lands, immense importance attaches to all Christian influences which can be brought to bear on the women, the mothers of the rising generation, and great is the difficulty of reaching them in the dreary homes in which, it is reckoned, that about 150,000,000 Chinese women of all ages live their monotonous lives in strict seclusion. Some of these patriarchal households number from sixty to one hundred women, ranging from great grandmothers down to their female slaves, and including the wives, widows, and other relations of father, sons, grandsons, and uncles. Of course, with the exception of the very few foreign ladies who have been able to make themselves acceptable to their Chinese sisters, no direct missionary influence can possibly find entrance within these jealously guarded homes, and the women's quarters are emphatically the great stronghold of that worship of their own ancestors, which is the main principle of Chinese life.*

It is the women who train their sons continually to offer worship and sacrifices to propitiate the dead, and whose vigorous denunciations have such weight with the husband, who (half disposed to become a Christian) is held back by the anger and despair of his women-folk at the thought of

---

* In my "Wanderings in China" (published by Blackwood), I have given very full details of this extraordinary system of religion, and of the manner in which it permeates every phase of Chinese life; also of some points of deep interest in the working of various Christian Missions, and I venture to ask all who are interested in the subject to refer to these chapters

his barbarously ceasing to offer the accustomed sacrifices to the dead. So until the women of China can be won for Christ, we can never hope for a very general conversion of the men.

And the great difficulty is to gain access to them. Foreign ladies are welcome, but not Chinese women of the lower classes, who form the bulk of the Christian converts, and consequently of the Bible-women.

When first Christian blind women had been taught to read, we trusted that they might prove valuable mission agents to their heathen sisters, as a blind Scripture reader would certainly be welcomed, were it only as a curiosity, to relieve the tedium of the dull day. But we quickly realized that this would not answer, as to send a blind woman alone into a heathen home would involve very grave peril to herself. Very likely she would never be taken into the women's quarters.

Then we supposed it was simply a question of expense, and that all would be well if we could secure an extra £10 a year to support a respectable sighted woman to take care of each blind reader. But it was soon found that reliable women are not to be had. None are available to whose charge a blind girl could safely be entrusted, so this phase of useful work cannot be developed till a longer course of Christian training has produced an altogether different code of morality.

When one thinks of the many thousands of blind girls and women in China, who could so easily be taught reading, writing, and to play the concertina as an accompaniment to the sacred lyrics which invariably prove so fascinating to Oriental ears, and when one realizes how welcome such teachers would be in the Zenanas, where the many million mothers of China are training their sons, it is distressing that this admirable work cannot be secured for the blind.

There is, however, good room for hope that when the extraordinary facility of Mr. Murray's Numeral Type for

Sighted persons becomes known, a great many sighted women, who can take care of themselves, will gain access to these homes, in order to teach ladies to read.

Chinese women are quite as intelligent as those of other lands, and though very few can read their own dull books, and much of their time is occupied in gossip, the care of their clothes, and ceaseless offerings of food and other gifts on the household altars, either to the gods or to their own ancestors, they can grasp a new idea, and ponder over it, and if it commends itself to them, they hold it with surprising tenacity, and endeavour to impress it on their neighbours. Hence it is that the staunch Chinese converts, both men and women, so frequently become active witnesses for the Truth.

It is scarcely to be expected that the Chinese themselves should make any special effort to send pupils to be trained at a school where every influence is used to convert the students to the Christian faith, and, as yet, no pupils of any social standing have availed themselves of Mr. Murray's tuition. Consequently, the average number of about fourteen lads continues to be recruited from the lowest of the people. Yet the wonderful rapidity with which those who are willing to be taught succeed in mastering the difficulties of reading, writing, and also of both writing and reading music, clearly proves how vast a field this work is destined to cover when once it becomes rightly known and understood in a land so slow to adopt any novelty.

Mr. Murray may be excused for a little pardonable pride in regard to lads who have been described as " salvage from the slums of Peking." "Now," he says, "it is a sight to see them at church. There are no Chinamen like them, so healthy, clean, and bright;" and several have already been sent forth thoroughly trained, to work under missionaries in other provinces.

Of course, it would be folly to expect that the flesh and the devil could allow so excellent a work to proceed unmarred, especially considering amid what utterly debasing influences most of these poor lads have hitherto lived. As regards blind adults, the majority are so utterly depraved that it is only in exceptional cases that Mr. Murray attempts to train one; and even these have, in several instances, caused him bitter disappointment, and he has, at various times, found it necessary for the good of all to expel both men and lads on whom he had lavished much care and patience.

But, then, the bright stars compensate for many sorrows.

Reviewing the work in the boys' school at the close of 1891, Mr. Murray says: "We have fifteen boys, and all are healthy and apt students. In addition to reading, writing, and music, they now learn geography and arithmetic. I have had a whole series of maps punched out on tin sheets, and the divisions numbered for convenient reference. The whole cost two dollars! The work was done by a needy scholar from a flooded part of the country. He first drew the outline on thin paper; this was pasted on to the tin sheet, with the drawing next to the tin. The lines thus reversed showed through sufficiently to guide the punch; thus they appear on the other side of the tin in raised outline, suitable for the blind pupils to finger."

The arithmetic lesson is wholly mental, and is taught by means of a *memoria technica* utterly perplexing to the foreign mind, but to the Chinese wondrously simple. Mr. Murray gives out long sentences, of which each word has a recognized equivalent in figures, and on the following day, solely from memory, the boys or girls give the result in a long, accurately worked-out sum—perhaps in compound multiplication.

He says: "I have prepared a little book on Mental Arithmetic by Mnemonics. The blind boys and girls have performed a feat by it. Every night for one week large sums were read out, as we would read out an anecdote, and on the following night the answer was given accurately, whether it was in addition, subtraction, division, or compound multiplication. The sums in addition had as many as ten lines of figures, all in thousands. One reading sufficed. Perhaps a boy read, and a girl translated the value. They went into it with such zest, that it was perfectly charming to me. No abacus needed!" (In Chinese shops the sighted tradesmen cannot, or will not, reckon the smallest account without calculating by means of an abacus, which is a wooden frame with moveable beads strung on wires.)

An extraordinary cultivation of the mechanical memory is one of the most striking characteristics of all Chinese education, so that an exercise which to us would be distasteful and laborious seems simple and easy to the Chinese, and most of all to the blind.

Certainly from the extraordinary powers of memory with which some of the students are endowed, it seems as though this special compensation was often bestowed on those who are deprived of the blessing of sight. Mr. Murray tells of one of his pupils who had not only written out St. Matthew's Gospel, but could repeat the whole perfectly by heart. Another had likewise committed to memory the whole of St. Mark. Others know every hymn in the hymn-books (one of which contains about one hundred and forty hymns and another four hundred).

The daily routine of learning goes on as already described, to the evident enjoyment of the students. All emboss from dictation, while to the more advanced workers is entrusted the stereotyping on brass sheets of pages of the Holy Scriptures. The Gospels have long been in circulation, each forming one concise volume such as the smallest lad can conveniently carry under his arm. Now the Book or Psalms and several more of the Old Testament and most of the Epistles are ready—others are in course of preparation.

On this subject Mr. Murray writes: "We do the work ourselves in school, stereotyping, printing, and binding, so it costs nothing, being done as part of the boys' course of lessons." Consequently, he is able to offer copies of each book for sale at an amazingly low price, as compared with that of books for the use of the blind embossed in this country. Sighted men have, however, to assist in embossing from the stereotyped sheets, and a reader has to go over all the work most carefully, as the arrangement of the verses is far more difficult to the blind than ordinary writing would be.

Six of the smallest boys are now daily sent to read the Holy Scriptures in the intervals between the daily services at several Mission chapels of various denominations in different parts of the city. These little lads read with the greatest coolness and courage, and with a fluency, accuracy, and excellent intonation to which Chinese scholars gifted with eyesight rarely attain in reading from their hieroglyphics, and many passers-by, who would never enter to hear foreign missionaries preach, pause wonderingly to watch these little lads read so admirably with the tips of their fingers, and some who can read the hieroglyphics buy copies of the Book that they may read it for themselves.

"Certainly God is blessing His Word in the mouth of these babes, who themselves seem to be really impressed with the responsibility and honour thus laid upon them, and nowhere is this more striking than at the hospital of the London Mission, where they read daily to an average of a hundred patients." Among these, considerable interest was aroused by William Burn's translation of "The Peep of Day." As the book had not at that time been embossed, the little reader wrote out one chapter every forenoon, and by eleven o'clock was ready to march off with it to the hospital, and there read it over and over again to successive groups of patients. Well might Mr. Murray say, "Could a sighted writer do more?" He continued: "If you could only hear how easily and fluently both boys and girls can read! it comes up to my brightest hopes. A young woman reads at our morning family prayers, and the little boys by turns in the evening. The other day Blind Peter was to give the address, so he asked a lad to read Romans iv. We could not but admire the speed and precision with which he read, and afterwards I made him read three chapters right through, while I took the time by my watch. The chapters I selected were the 3rd, 4th, and 5th. He took exactly four and a half minutes to the 3rd, the same to the 4th, and five minutes to the last. Nothing could be more desirable than that! I feel a great delight in mentioning this, for I never in Edinburgh or Glasgow heard anything like it, and I am sure that nothing could surpass this. Think how the fingers look to see this! they seem hardly to touch the paper, but glide over the page like those of a skilled player over the key-board of a piano!

"After sending the boy back to school, I read the same chapters while Mrs. Murray held the watch. I read as quickly as people usually read the sacred volume, and the time I took was as nearly as possible the same. I consider it a triumph that the Chinese boy without eyes should be able to read as quickly as I did with eyes!"

One difficulty in a city of such enormous distances as Peking is, that it would be impossible for these little blind lads to walk daily to their respective reading-stations, so it is necessary to hire one of the curious Chinese carts to carry them. Mr. Murray justly observed that it would be cheaper, as well as more convenient, to have a van and horse belonging to the Mission.

He also pointed out how very desirable it was that the Mission should possess an infirmary, on however humble a scale, so as to make it possible to isolate cases of infectious illness, to which all must be liable in the heart of such a city as Peking. The need for such an asylum was sorely proved when a very promising pupil died of consumption, and a little blind girl was seriously ill with typhus fever, at the very time when Mrs. Murray herself, and also a young blind married woman, required the utmost care and quiet. And all this within the confined space of a small Chinese court! At another time scarlet fever was so rife in the city that funerals were constantly passing along the street. There were two cases in the Blind School, causing great anxiety lest the infection should spread, and many a wish for the isolation of the patients.

In 1890 there were trials of various sorts—incursions of thieves, serious sickness in the city, a succession of dust storms, and of such appalling rains as flooded vast districts of the Empire. Though Peking suffered less than many other places, great damage was done, and the inmates of the Blind Schools had their full share of anxiety and trouble.

Letters from Mr. Murray and others told how a summer of almost unprecedented heat (resulting in a grievous epidemic of typhoid fever) was followed by terrible and prolonged tempests, with incessant rain. Every mountain streamlet was transformed into a raging torrent—whole villages were swept away, leaving scarce a trace of what, a few hours earlier, had been flourishing communities—fertile plains, richly clothed with millet and other crops, became the bed of wide lakes, whose surging waters carried sudden death and destruction to many a peaceful homestead.

In the city of Peking there was widespread ruin and many lives lost, as on every side mud walls crumbled, heavy thatched or tiled roofs gave way, as the timbers which had upheld them fell crashing to the ground.

Within the School for the Blind Mr. Murray kept anxious watch, his care being divided between his helpless blind charges and his own family—his wife's nervous system having quite broken down under such prolonged tension following immediately after the birth of her second child.

There was also grave anxiety on account of several colporteurs, who had been sent with a supply of books for sale in the country. These latter eventually returned in safety (having, however, been obliged to abandon their cart); but, to quote Mr. Murray's words, "both carters and mules looked but the ghosts of their former selves. The sights they have seen, of ruin and distress, would fill a volume." They had to ford fourteen streams, each of which had become a rushing river, so that they were repeatedly in imminent danger, the mules sinking and tumbling, stupefied with fright, and the men often breast-deep in the flood. The most extraordinary thing was, that under such very adverse circumstances and with rain falling incessantly, they should have succeeded in selling nearly 1000 copies of the Holy Scriptures.

Mr. Murray told how, day by day, as portions of his walls and ceilings fell, he shifted his pupils, their books and furniture, from one corner to another, covering them up as best he could, but living in the ceaseless expectation of a total collapse.

One horribly suggestive detail in the story of their miseries was the overflow of the city sewers, which flooded the school, of course totally destroying all the mats and whatever else was touched by that foul stream. The subsequent cleansing of the premises was very troublesome work, especially as every neighbour was in the same plight, and it would have been marvellous indeed if a renewed epidemic of fever had not ensued.

Notwithstanding his splendid faculty for accepting all life's trials as blessings in disguise, Mr. Murray confessed that it was not easy to be philosophical when the house was tumbling piecemeal, and when, day and night, he was expecting a crash.

Of course there was no chance of any help in China, where all were paralyzed by the magnitude of the disasters which had overwhelmed such vast districts in so many Provinces. In the country around Peking and Tientsin alone, the official report stated that upwards of 1000 villages had been destroyed—in some cases swept away, with all their inhabitants, none surviving to tell the tale, while 4,000,000 persons were left absolutely destitute. Even when the flood had begun to abate, the waters still covered an expanse of fully 3000 square miles of what was fertile and densely-populated land, and it was estimated that even if the waters received no fresh accession, it would be about three years before they ran off sufficiently to allow of cultivating the soil.

Under these circumstances it was evident that there was very special need for immediate pecuniary aid to enable Mr. Murray to rebuild his schools, and I earnestly appealed to the public to give practical proof of sympathy by sending a donation, AS A THANK-OFFERING FOR THEIR OWN COMFORTABLE HOMES.

I am sorry to say that the response was so meagre that it only sufficed to patch up the dilapidated old Chinese houses, and from that day to this (October, 1897) the summer rains have each year proved a season of grave danger and anxiety—far more so than the snows and tempests of winter—and each season has necessitated serious repairs.

In August, 1893, Mr. Murray wrote from the American and Presbyterian Sanatorium, in the Western Hills, to which he had happily removed his children : " The storms of the season for the third consecutive year have been very severe indeed. Even here the houses seemed to totter with the vehemence of the rain. Think of one downpour lasting without cessation for three days and three nights! All the houses leaked, and a wall of one fell during the night.

" But what of our house in the city ? As soon as the storm abated, I rode into the city—no easy matter, the roads being now rivers. The mud in many of the streets is literally two feet deep, with here and there great holes into which mules and carts tumble helplessly. Arrived ! Ah me ! Desolation—ceilings all down, or parts hanging in tatters. Furniture soaked, as also my favourite book-case and all my books—my Hebrew, Greek and Latin commentaries. Every part of the house leaked—the shop, the blind men's room, the book-room, the printing-room; of the latter, the outer half of the wall fell, as also part of the roof of our sitting-room. The only places that resisted are the Boys' School and the room which I built out of the wreck of last year. Everywhere the smells are putrid."

Two months later he wrote: "The rainy season began a month earlier than usual and is only just over. Even now, some streets are not passable. The schools had a longer holiday than usual on this account, but now we have all work going forward." Throughout this interval he was very ill from being obliged to live in the soaking ruins, inhaling the pestilential miasma. For one thing, he developed a racking cough and cold, and greatly alarmed his doctor by spitting blood. Happily his work on earth was still unfinished, and he made a strangely rapid recovery. His wife returned from the hills that she might personally superintend the Chinese masons, joiners and coolies who were patching up the ruins to make them once more habitable.

In June, 1894, he wrote: "I have had masons at work for a month patching up the roofs, in the hope of enabling them to stand the strain of another year's storms, just at hand. The mason, who is an elder of the London Mission, is doing the work well. But there are two parts liable to tumble; one of these is our bed-room, unless we can get at the decayed pillar and renew the foot, which will not be easy, as the wall is already split, and to touch it may bring it all down, and the roof at the same time." (A pleasant house in which to face vehement and tempestuous winds and storms!) "This is the broiling season. It is very unhealthy in the city, as more drains are being opened this year. Fever is very prevalent. Two missionaries are down with it."

In August he told us how the cobbled-up houses had stood the dangers. "The rains have not been so savage as those of '92 and '93, but have been more constant, and continue longer. The city is a picture of distress, like a saturated sponge. The heat has been very great. I am glad to say the Christian mason made so good a job of repairing our roofs that they have held tight, except in one part which leaked, and there the ceiling came down with a crash beside my bed, and awoke me with a start. Still, the old beams are so risky, and all the woodwork so rotten, and a great smash is so probable, that it was a comfort to have the children in safety at the Mission station in the hills. The great heat and damp try the strongest constitution. One week back in the city seems to have undone all the good, for the children (who were looking so well) now look sickly, and suffer much from diarrhœa, &c. Everything smells damp and sickly. The very typewriter is sick. The type-plate has stretched, and lies on the ink-plate, stiff and hard to work, and prints the letters out of line. I hope it will recover when dry weather comes."

But I am running on too fast, and must return to the School as it was in 1890. Amongst other disappointments it was deemed desirable to send three adult pupils back to their villages. Two were men over forty years of age, whose progress was slow, and who sometimes found it difficult to conform to the discipline of the school. Two very promising lads died.

Mr. Murray speaks sorrowfully of many such disappointments. He says: "Death has been such an enemy to our success. It has seemed like educating them for Heaven, and as soon as they are fully equipped, off they go! I fear this is not my wish! We would like them to be spared to do some work here first. But the LORD means otherwise."

In one year three of his advanced students died: all of them lads who, in addition to other acquirements, were able to stereotype well. All three had returned to their respective homes, apparently suffering only from a slight cold, but in each case rapid consumption set in and soon proved fatal. The young brother of one of these, a lad aged 14, remained in the school, a good student, and one of the chapel readers, but the doctor says this insidious disease is in his blood also, so he is soon likely to follow. All possible care is taken of the poor lads, physically as well as morally, but consumption seems to be exceedingly common among the Chinese, especially the blind, and Mr. Murray learns that other schools have a like experience.

A very disappointing instance of this was the death of a blind man in the Province of Shantung, who was unable to come to Peking to be taught. The missionary who had advised him to do so then sent to Mr. Murray for a Primer and a writing-frame, and having commenced by himself mastering the system, he straightway set to work to teach the blind man, succeeding so well that he felt assured that his pupil would prove of real use, when alas! this apt scholar sickened and died. The facility with which the teacher taught himself with only the aid of the Primer, was a satisfactory reply to some who raised objections to the system, on the ground of its being so perplexing!

Amongst many who have given practical proof of this facility, I may mention Miss Sheckleton, who brought a blind girl from Shansi Province, to be trained as a teacher. During the few days she herself remained in Peking, she went round the other Missions to see their work, and then went to the Blind Girls' School to get a lesson herself. After the second lesson she said, "Now I do not require another word of instruction! I know my way." She then settled down to work, and, after two or three days, was able to write quite clearly. She then started on her return journey, studying hard all the time.

As a striking instance of the rapidity with which a really intelligent blind pupil, anxious to learn, can acquire Mr. Murray's system, he mentions Mr. P'an, the Blind Evangelist trained for the Rev. Mr. Keer, of the Irish Mission at Niu Chwang. On the two first days after his arrival, Mr. Murray devoted two hours each morning to teaching him. On the third morning he repeated the whole of the lessons and the thirty Braille symbols employed in reading.

Of this earnest student Mr. Keer wrote that his reading and effective speaking were a marvel to the people, and that his life was to the glory of GOD. But sad to say, his career of usefulness was very soon cut short by the dread cholera, which claimed him as a victim.

Even quite young boys sometimes master the system effectually in five days, and can then gradually, by practice, acquire speed in reading and writing. At the present moment (1897) there is in the school a little chap, only seven years old, who did this in ten days, though the poor little fellow's progress was somewhat impeded by an occasional breakdown, crying for his parents.

As an instance of a man blind from his birth or childhood, who grew up steeped in all the evil common to his class, and nevertheless has turned out a thoroughly satisfactory convert, I may mention one specially dear to Mr. Murray— namely, Mr. Hsii, who, *from the first time he had a chance of hearing the Gospel preached*, became truly converted. He had been a fortune-teller, and a man of immoral character. He sought medical advice at the London Mission Hospital, where he heard the Gospel preached, and was converted.

Owing to the nature of his disease, he could not be received at the Blind School, but being remarkably intelligent, he rapidly mastered the Primer with the aid of a sighted boy, who had learned it in order to acquire Mr. Murray's system of shorthand writing. Then he returned to the school to crave a lesson in fingering, and gave such convincing proof of his earnest desire to live a new life, that Mr. Murray undertook to teach him.

"I sinned," he said, "because I did not know GOD.

Henceforth I desire to serve HIM only, and to be able to read HIS WORD."

By the fifth day he could finger so freely that he was able to read two chapters of Romans correctly, and within a fortnight he was brought before the Peking Board of Directors of the school, and read several passages correctly. Someone dictated a very out-of-the-way sentence, which he wrote, and then a blind boy was called in from the school, and at once read it correctly.

His heathen relations, who foresaw the loss of considerable gain in his giving up fortune-telling, did all in their power to prevent his doing so; his step-father captured and beat him, stripping him of all the clothes given him at the Mission, except one light garment. But Hsii stood firm, and made his way back to his friends, and, ere long, was admitted to baptism. Thenceforward his chief desire has been to tell the story of the Cross, and to read the Bible to those who formerly paid to hear such different stories from him, and now come to hear "without money and without price."

As a beginning of work he was provided with a table and two folding stools, for himself and his companion, and he sat in the street, reading. (The 10*l.* a year requisite for his maintenance was provided by a friend in Prince Edward's Island.)

He was a skilful player on the Chinese guitar, banjo, and dulcimer; now he can also play on the piano and the American organ, and it is hoped that he will gain admission to the homes of the well-to-do class who have blind sons wishing to be taught.

Having received a request from the missionary in charge of the American Presbyterian Mission at Nanking, to send him an organist who was also thoroughly acquainted with the various developments of the Numeral Type, Mr. Murray selected Hsii for the post.

He wrote: "Hsii is a capable fellow, and well able to do

us credit. He can play hundreds of tunes on his various instruments. He speaks well, and reads touchingly. He can teach reading, writing, and shorthand, both to the blind and the sighted. I know, if God keep him, he will be a treasure to a Mission."

Soon he received letters cordially commending Hsii and his musical and other talents, and Mr. Murray hoped that his Numeral Type was now securely started at Nanking,* " the Southern Capital." But other influences had been at work, and the advocates of another system for teaching the blind prevailed, so Hsii was sent back to Peking, much to Mr. Murray's disappointment. He is now working in Peking as a colporteur under the Rev. George Owen, and is organist at the London Mission Chapel in the East City, where he gives the utmost satisfaction.

Perhaps the most strikingly interesting of Mr. Murray's pupils is Mr. Ch'ang, a blind man from Manchuria, that vast Province to the extreme north-east, just north of Korea, and which (like that strange Hermit Kingdom) was, till quite recently, untouched by missionary effort, except a small Roman Catholic Mission. At last a beginning was made by the establishment of a Presbyterian Medical Mission at Moukden, the capital—which is a city of about 250,000 inhabitants—a tiny light kindled in the midst of the great idolatrous city, and so rapid has been the spread of interest and inquiry, that it is difficult to believe that Manchuria actually forms part of ultra-conservative China.

The simple story of Ch'ang's conversion is, in itself, an all-sufficient answer to those who are disposed to cavil at the slow return of missionary efforts. He was a member of the Hun Yuen, a very zealous sect of Buddhists. They are vegetarians, abstaining from both flesh and wine. They form one of the numerous secret societies of China, and are hence suspected by the Government as dangerous. They

* Nanking—*Nan*, South ; *king*, Capital. Peking—*Pĕ*, North ; *king*, Capital.

have initiatory rites which are as secret as those of Freemasonry. The members of this society are generally earnest and devout, and when really converted they become most uncompromising Christians. Two-thirds of the converts in Manchuria, to the north of Moukden, belong to the Hun Yuen.

Ch'ang was intellectually a seeker after truth wherever he could find it, and was well versed in the teachings of Confucius as well as those of Buddha. But these cold systems failed to touch his heart or control his life, and he was known as an inveterate gambler.

In 1886, when he was about thirty-seven years of age, his sight began to fail, and it became rapidly worse.

In his remote mountain village of Tai-ping-kou, he heard rumours of wonderful cures wrought at Moukden by Dr. Christie, at the Medical Mission of the United Presbyterian Church. So in his dreary darkness he groped his way for more than a hundred miles to place himself under his care, hoping that he too might have his sight restored.

He had sold what little property he possessed to pay his gambling debts, and carried with him the small surplus in order to pay for his lodgings in the city; but alas! he fell among thieves, who robbed him of everything, and left him to starve.

With increased difficulty he continued his journey, and one morning a poor blind man, clothed only in a few rags, and apparently in the last stage of dysentery, was found at the gate of the Mission Hospital. Every bed was full, but the native Evangelist offered to give up his own, in order that this poor sufferer might receive the best possible nursing. Never was care better rewarded.

Ere long Ch'ang's health was restored, and as regards sight, a partial cure was effected, so that he could see a little. But soon after he left the hospital a Chinese friend assured him that he could greatly improve the sight by inserting a needle into the eye, an operation to which poor

Ch'ang unfortunately submitted, with the result that he was thenceforth totally and incurably blind.

But the Christian teaching which he heard at once struck home, and took root in his innermost heart. He had long before selected for himself all that was best in the teaching of Buddha and Confucius, but now he recognized that what he had been ignorantly feeling after was the knowledge of a personal Saviour, and from the moment he heard of the LORD JESUS, he at once accepted and enthroned HIM as his own Lord and Master.

Ere a month had expired he asked to be admitted to Christian baptism. With what seems an excess of caution, his teacher deemed it right to insist on a period of probation. Truly touching was the blind man's reply. "NONE OF MY PEOPLE HAVE EVER HEARD EVEN THE NAME OF JESUS, OR OF HIS OFFER OF A GIFT OF ETERNAL LIFE, AND DO YOU THINK I CAN KEEP THAT TO MYSELF ANY LONGER? I do wish for baptism, but I cannot delay my return." So poor blind Ch'ang was dismissed without this outward sign of his new faith, only with a promise that ere long his friend, the Rev. James Webster, would follow and seek him in his mountain village.

But there were at that time only three missionaries in Moukden, and the multitude of cares and pressure of work proved more than they could meet, so that six months elapsed ere Mr. Webster was able to redeem his promise, and then had considerable difficulty in reaching this remote village. He was much surprised, however, in a country where blindness is common, to find how well known this poor blind man seemed to be; and when at length he reached the village of which he was in search, and which apparently had never been visited by any foreigner, instead of being received with the usual shouts of "foreign devil," he was cordially welcomed by Mr. Li, the village schoolmaster, who expressed his pleasure that "the pastor had at length arrived," and told him how Ch'ang had gone forth on what, since his return from Moukden, had been his daily occupation, namely, that of travelling from village to village (across the muddy swamps and over the steep hill paths, which had proved so difficult and wearisome to the foreigner gifted with sight), in order to tell the people about "this religion of Jesus," sometimes in the evenings having hundreds of hearers beneath the shade of the willow trees, or getting smaller congregations in such houses as would receive him.

At first everyone laughed at him, or pitied him, thinking him crazy, but after awhile, as he persevered and gave practical proof of true holiness of life, public opinion became divided. Some were for him and some against him; some blessed him, some cursed him. But week after week the blind man persevered, daily praying for help from on high, never weary of singing the one hymn he had been taught in the hospital, "This I know, that Jesus loves me," and then going forth alone, groping his darkened way with his staff, and ceaselessly telling to all who would listen, the good news of ETERNAL LIFE BY JESUS CHRIST.

"And the result of all this," said Mr. Li (who himself was Ch'ang's first convert), "is that a large number earnestly inquired about his 'doctrine,' and heartily believe, and desire to become members of the religion of Jesus."

Presently Ch'ang himself returned, and his joy on hearing of his friend's arrival was most pathetic. Tears dropped from his sightless eyes as he exclaimed (in a manner which clearly proved how many had scoffed at the blind man's faith in his friend's promise)—"O pastor, I always said you WOULD come!" Very quickly he despatched messengers to various villages, whence his converts soon arrived, and these, one by one, in the simplest language, and with an indescribable warmth of feeling and earnestness of purpose, gave expression to a faith so unmistakably genuine, that on the morrow nine of them, headed by their sightless teacher, received that holy baptism which all fully recognized as the outward symbol of a faith exposing those who profess it to the chance of persecution even unto death, in such horrid forms as has recently been the lot of many of China's martyrs. Several others likewise desired to be baptized, but were required to wait for fuller instruction.

"One thing of which I am well assured," says Mr. Webster, "is this: Blind Ch'ang, of Tai-ping-kow, with little knowledge, but with a heart thrilled to the core with the truth which he knew, had in these months done more work and better work for the kingdom of heaven than half-a-dozen foreign missionaries could have done in as many years. And this is only one of many proofs that China must be evangelized by the Chinese."

Ch'ang confided to his friend that he had been greatly helped and comforted by a dream which he had one night soon after leaving the Mission; he had been groping along the mountain paths from one village inn to another, telling his wonderful story to his fellow-wayfarers wherever he spent the night, till wearied nature claimed her rest. Then, in a glorious vision, he beheld the Saviour robed in white, and crowned with dazzling light. He came towards him with a Book in His hand, and, smiling upon him, HE gave him the Book and straightway vanished.

His friend told him that the Vision was to be literally fulfilled, for that the WORD of GOD was now given to the Blind, and that if he aspired to teach others, he must learn to read the Book himself. That for this purpose he must go to Peking, and there place himself as a student in the School for the Blind.

Naturally the idea that he could ever be taught to read and write seemed to Ch'ang like a fable. Nevertheless, to please his friend, he promised to do his best, and so, accompanied by a delicate blind lad, whose friends wished him also to acquire this wonderful knowledge, he started on the long and difficult journey. First, the hundred miles on foot across the mountains to Moukden. Then by boat down the river to Niu Chwang, where he must secure a passage across the Yellow Sea to the mouth of the Peiho river. Then another two or three days' journey by boat to Tung-chow, whence a cart would convey him to Peking. All these troublesome

CH'ANG, THE BLIND APOSTLE OF MANCHURIA.

changes the blind man faced, though with small hope of any such blessed result as success.

Warmly was he greeted and welcomed by Mr. Murray, and, to his own infinite surprise, within three months he had so thoroughly mastered the arts of reading and writing, and also of writing and reading music, that he was able to take a pupil and instruct him in all these arts.

Fain would Mr. Murray have detained him to receive a lengthened course of tuition, but the continued illness of the blind lad, of whom he had undertaken charge, and the opportunity of a return voyage for both, down the Peiho to Tientsin for a dollar apiece, by a boat which had brought stores for the Mission, added to his longing to begin at once imparting all his new knowledge to his countrymen, decided Ch'ang to return at once, though grieving sorely to tear himself away from his friends, especially from Blind Peter, who had been his special teacher.

"Three months ago," he said, "I came, though believing it to be impossible for a blind man to learn to read and write. Now, praise God for His wonders to me! I can read and write anything, and instead of having to remember all as a burden on my memory, I have several books which I have written out myself. But my countrymen are all heathen, and I must go and show them what the Lord has done for me, and preach His blessed Gospel to them."

He was provided with such portions of the Holy Scriptures as had then been stereotyped by the blind students at the Peking school, and with a new writing-frame; and soon Mr. Murray was gladdened by a letter in embossed type from Ch'ang himself, who, with the delicate blind lad as his constant and devoted companion, had recommenced his daily itinerating, reading the Holy Word to all the wondering crowds who assembled to see a blind man read with the tips of his fingers.

It was in 1886 that Ch'ang paid this, his first visit, to Peking. About the close of 1890 he returned thither for further instruction on various points, and ever since then he has continued working zealously as a pioneer in different parts of the Manchurian mountains. At one time he reached a district fully two hundred miles further east, and there began a work which has prospered year by year. At the present moment whole communities are earnestly seeking further teaching, regarding the truths first declared so energetically by this earnest preacher. One of these enquirers said, "Had Ch'ang never become blind, there might have been no Christians here yet."

Of course when more advanced teaching is required, it is evident that such pioneers as Ch'ang must be reinforced and supported by the foreign missionaries, who can keep a guiding hand and act as chief shepherds of the flock. In his case the very natural danger has been lest he should mix up his old dreams of attaining perfection by his own efforts with the simpler teachings of Scripture.

As an instance of the very varied class of men who have been converted through Ch'ang's instrumentality, I may quote part of a letter from the Rev. John Ross, D.D., after a visit to Tai-ping-kow in 1890. He says: "One of those baptized, named Lin, was at one time a highway robber. He was also a heavy opium-smoker, and guilty of most of the vices of vicious China. His was a decided case of thorough conversion. A look into the man's face showed what a change had come over him.

"Next to him stood a native doctor, close upon seventy years of age, who had come from a long distance to ask for baptism. He had heard the story of the Cross from an old member. He wondered whether it was possible that GOD could display such mercy as to forgive the sins of a lifetime. Simple-minded as a child, this man received the truth with joy.

"Beside him was a man, named Chao, who had from youth up earnestly sought after truth. He had become a strict ascetic at an early age, and always meditated on 'The True.' His influence afterwards became so great that over a thousand disciples followed his lead, and practised the same austerities and religious forms. His word with them was law." (He was the local leader of the Hun Yuen sect.) "A more modest man I have not met in Manchuria, nor a man who had dived so deep into the treasures of truth. The questions which he constantly presented showed him to be a profound thinker. His one great regret was that he had led so many men in search of peace 'on the wrong way.' Most of his disciples are well to do, and he loses a large income by becoming a Christian.

"Close by this man stood a youth of twenty-two, a disciple of the last mentioned. His father is one of the largest land owners in that region. His parents were quite willing that he should be baptized, being themselves secret believers ; also disciples of Chao.

"The fifth was a blind man, formerly a schoolmaster, whose peace of mind was well displayed in a face always shining with the light within. Before a year is over, each of these will have his own fruit borne, in bringing others in.

"There was, in all, a company of twenty-four believers, who met twice daily for Christian instruction. They certainly seemed like thirsty ground drinking in the refreshing rain. For an hour each time I spoke on some Christian Truth, and when done, I was plied with questions to elicit further instruction."

In the following year the Rev. James Webster again visited this district, i.e. Tai-ping-kow and Mai-mai-gai, and found " Ch'ang looking stout and ruddy, as if his frequent fastings had done him no harm." He says : "Where six years ago we stood and viewed the wide surrounding country wholly given to idolatry, without a single believer, there are now upwards of 150 baptized converts, and as many more who believe, and who will ere long proclaim themselves for Christ. But that does not tell half the story of blessing, for from that valley rays of Gospel light have streamed out to other villages which were sitting in darkness, but are now rejoicing in the Light. Many are the imperfections of the converts, and great is their need for further instruction, but their work has been wonderfully owned of GOD. Truly this is the LORD's doing, and it is marvellous in our eyes."

In the autumn of 1892 (a year of bitter persecution and widespread anxiety, especially unfavourable to the extension of Mission work) Ch'ang's converts were found to number considerably over three hundred souls, of whom more than half had been admitted to baptism, the others being still on probation. About three years later we heard that fully five hundred of those who had been baptized owed their conversion, humanly speaking, to Ch'ang's preaching.

In these early years he was well helped by his first convert, Mr. Li, who likewise was unwearied in his zeal, preaching and teaching in all the surrounding villages. Naturally enough his school was deserted by his former scholars, and for awhile he had to leave his own village.

In the summer of 1897 Mr. Webster thus sums up the results of Ch'ang's preaching :—

"The work in Mai-mai-gai was certainly begun by him, and so we may say that indirectly the Church in that region owes its existence, under GOD, to blind Ch'ang. Several years ago he went to another district, 200 miles further east, and began a work there which has prospered year by year, and is one of our most hopeful stations at the present moment. Ch'ang has his failings like everybody else, but take him all round, there is no more earnest or successful lay Evangelist in Manchuria, or one who has been more blessed of GOD in winning men to Christ. Hundreds in Manchuria owe their Christian faith to his direct agency, and hundreds more are in the Church to-day as the fruits of the seed he was privileged to sow. HE HAS BEEN THE MEANS OF WINNING MORE MEN FOR CHRIST THAN ANY OTHER MAN I KNOW."

It seems to me that in all its details this story is strikingly characteristic of the methods most frequently chosen by GOD for the extension of His Kingdom. Not by human might, nor by human power, but by the influence of His

Holy Spirit working through what to us seem such humble agencies. Here we have a chain of events by which two men (one called from his father's saw-mill in Glasgow by a distressing accident which left him crippled for life; the other from his father's corn-mill at Auchintoul, near Banff, to very special lines of mission-work in two of the chief cities of China), though personally unknown to one another, were each led to take part in the conversion and training of one poor, recently-blinded Chinaman, whom GOD was preparing in His own way for unique work as a pioneer in a great heathen Province—work which has been so honoured by the MASTER, that Ch'ang has been well described as "The Blind Apostle of Manchuria."

Close to that old mill of Auchintoul there is a wood which to me suggests very strikingly the analogy between the visible and the spiritual worlds—the natural spreading of plants, and the growth of the Kingdom of Heaven.

About a quarter of a century ago, there was brought to the garden of the old house of Auchintoul a plant of large blue forget-me-not, transplanted from a distant part of England. The little exile took so kindly to its new soil that in a very few years superfluous plants were thrown out into the wood, and seeds found their way to the neighbouring glen, where they found congenial nestling-places all along the banks of a streamlet, whence they spread in every direction, till now the ground is carpeted with their luxuriant growth, and in the sweet summer time the shady wood is blue with the lovely blossoms. And all this beauty has been derived from one small seedling transplanted from its early home in Yorkshire.

In like manner a son of that old mill was guided to far Manchuria, where for several anxious years, he and two or three earnest fellow-workers toiled all unknown amongst the surrounding millions of Heathen in a vast famine-stricken region—a position which might well discourage the stoutest heart. Yet he may have found a cheering gleam of promise in remembering the spreading of the blue flowerets through the wood beside the old home—and certain it is that already these early sowers of the Word in Manchuria are being privileged to gather in a harvest beyond their most sanguine hopes. Dr. Ross writes concerning this: "The vast change from hostility to indifference, and now to deep interest, is to me amazing."

I have told how Mr. Webster persuaded Ch'ang to take the long journey to Peking in order to be taught by Mr. Murray. Though very early impressed by a conviction of the value of Mr. Murray's inventions, he had never met him. I must now tell of the assuredly Providential Guiding which led him to visit the School for the Blind at Peking, in the spring of 1897.

In the beginning of the year, a lady who had been urged to take a more definite interest in furthering Murray's system, had replied that she would do so if she received from Mr. Webster and Dr. Ross of Manchuria, satisfactory accounts of its practical working. She accordingly wrote to these missionaries, and at once received from the latter a letter of warmest commendation thereof.

Mr. Webster had just started on a brief furlough to Scotland, and being anxious to arrive in time for the General Assembly in Edinburgh, he and his wife took the circuitous and troublesome land journey to Tientsin, which is the Port of Peking, hoping that as the ice there melts earlier than it does in Manchuria, they might there find a homeward-bound steamer. On arriving there, however, they found the Peiho still ice-bound, necessitating a delay of two weeks. Meanwhile Mr. Webster had received the lady's letter, and at once resolved to utilize his enforced detention by a visit to Peking, involving a three days' journey in a terribly jolting cart. But all the hard bumps were forgotten in the joy with which Mr. Murray welcomed his unexpected guests. About a week was devoted to close study of the system in all its details, and thus

Mr. Webster was able not only to reply from personal knowledge to one enquirer, but became an enthusiastic witness in favour of Mr. Murray and his work, to as many as he could interest in the subject during his too brief stay in Scotland.

Ch'ang's pioneer work has naturally attracted the notice of missionaries in Manchuria to the training of the blind, both for their own benefit and as valuable agents for spreading the truth.

Dr. Brander, of the Irish Presbyterian Medical Mission in Manchuria, was one of the first to send pupils to be trained by Mr. Murray, that they might return as teachers.

The first tiny school for the blind at Moukden was commenced by Tiao, a lad sent by Mr. Webster to Peking, there to be trained by Mr. Murray as an organist. He remained at the school about two years (till 1892), and was subsequently sent back for further training in the art of teaching others. His return was delayed owing to the outbreak of war in Manchuria, so that ere he left Peking he was thoroughly instructed in reading and writing, vocal and instrumental music, and had fingered his way through almost all the books in stock, stereotyped or hand-written, as also all the music. Best of all, he had been so long in personal contact with Mr. Murray that he was thoroughly under his good influence, and able to train others on the same lines.

Of this lad, the Rev. John Ross, D.D., writes: "The blind have most extraordinary memories. Tiao leads the psalmody in church, having learned to play accurately over three hundred tunes. I have on several occasions translated a tune for him into the Tonic sol-fa system. He has written down treble and bass successively, and then, laying down the paper on which he had written it out, he played the tune on the American organ. Only once did he make one mistake, which was corrected and never repeated."

Other missionaries have referred to their surprise when asked to take the service in one of the churches where the organist is blind, and being told to give out any hymn they fancied, without any previous reference to the accompanist. Perhaps they gave out such a number as 396 or 421, and then noted how the blind man seemed to think for a few seconds, and then invariably struck up the right tune. Of course their memory is greatly assisted by Mr. Murray's system of mnemonics.

Still more surprising is the memory of Blind Ch'ang, who now knows by heart the whole of the New Testament, the Psalms, and several other books of the Old Testament, and can quote them with such extraordinary accuracy that if you mention any chapter and ask him to repeat from, say, the fourth to the end of the seventeenth verse, he at once begins at the right verse, and quotes faultlessly to the exact word indicated.

Tiao's school was started with three boys, fine-looking little fellows, blinded by small-pox. Within two months one of these could read so fluently that he was ready to teach others, and Dr. Ross was already looking forward to their starting schools in at least half a dozen different districts, all to be taught by Tiao's pupils. The latter already included some bright young men with sight, who perceived how valuable the system would be to them as scholars in taking notes.

Of course the difficulty in starting schools in Manchuria, as in all other Provinces, is lack of funds, as the pupils are almost invariably quite destitute—blind members of even respectable families being required to earn their own living as professional fortune-tellers. Dr. Ross estimates that in Manchuria ten blind lads might possibly be lodged, fed and clothed for £50 a year. He hopes that ere long many such Messengers of the Cross will be trained to go forth over the country as bearers of Good Tidings.

He says: "OF THE SUPERIORITY OF MURRAY'S SYSTEM TO ANY OTHER I HAVE NO DOUBT, as it is in reality a shorthand system. IT DESERVES THE SUPPORT OF EVERY PHILANTHROPIST, AND THE PRAYERS OF EVERY CHRISTIAN."

PART II.

EASY READING FOR ILLITERATE SIGHTED CHINESE.

FOR the first ten years from the invention of the Numeral Type in 1879, it was essentially WORK FOR THE BLIND, and not even Mr. Murray himself suspected that THIS WAS ONLY THE INITIAL STAGE, or, as he loves to call it, "his First Revelation." The Second, which is of infinitely wider importance, is the natural development of the first, namely THE APPLICATION OF THE SELF-SAME SYSTEM TO THE USE OF THE SIGHTED, BY CONNECTING WITH VISIBLE BLACK LINES THE EMBOSSED WHITE DOTS PREPARED ONLY FOR THE FINGERS OF THE BLIND.

It was about the close of 1889 that someone said to Mr. Murray, half in jest, "Oh, what a privilege it is to be blind, and to learn to read and write well in a few weeks, whereas sighted persons take about six years to learn to read very imperfectly, and even then cannot write at all. Why don't you do something for poor sighted persons?"

Then his friend, Mrs. Blodget (wife of the Rev. H. Blodget, D.D., of the American Congregational Mission), suggested that surely the system which proved so simple for the Blind, would be equally so for the sighted if they could see it. Then he bethought him of using visible black lines instead of white dots, and thus produced a series of squares and angles, forming the simplest set of symbols in existence.

Here are specimens of these different styles of writing.

Embossed for the blind.

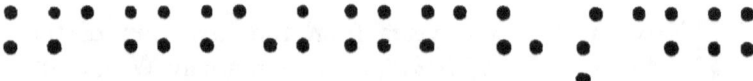

Printed in black for the sighted, by filling in the outline of the points.

Shorthand of the above.

Cut style, without tones.

He at once wrote out lessons in these with his tiny paintbrush, in order to test whether illiterate sighted persons could recognize them, and to his great joy he succeeded in teaching several to read in less than a week. The next anxiety was to get metal types for printing prepared; but now there ensued a series of those tantalizing delays which have proved so sorely trying to even this most patient of men at every successive stage of his work. More than two precious years were lost ere he was able to get this simple type and so turn his invention to practical account.

First he appealed to his friends in this country to have the type prepared, but needless to say, his requirements were not understood, and met with no response. Then he prepared small models of all the symbols, and a Chinaman cut exact copies of these in wood, from which Mr. Archibald, of the National Bible Society's printing-press at Hankow, prepared matrices, and was ready to produce the much-desired type, when the order for its preparation was cancelled, because some members of Mr. Murray's own Home Committee considered that this was not a legitimate use of money given to develop his inventions for the Blind. Three years later, when in dire anxiety lest a Roman alphabetic system should be adopted in many districts, he says: "If only I had a private income, the Numeral Type would have been started three years ago. The fault of slow results is not in myself!"*

* The incessant thwarting by which at every step this work has been hindered and delayed, has really seemed to justify the remark of one who said we could not have a better proof of its real value, than the fact that Satan seems to be continually on the alert to hinder it in every detail, and again and again on some painful pretext, to stir up opposition from most unexpected quarters.

Think of the many months that must elapse between the date of his writing from Peking to Scotland for something imperatively needed, and then when at last the answer is due, to find that it is only a request for further instructions, or possibly a refusal! Too often a long expected treasure arrives sadly damaged, as was the case with a valuable stereotype-maker, the cost of which was collected by a blind friend in America. A typewriter from Scotland arrived *minus* essential parts, and when after more than a year's delay the omission was rectified, the long looked-for package was never received. 1897 is now nearing its close, and Mr. Murray has vainly waited for a first-class printing-press promised in 1895. And so the tale of long-tried patience goes on, while the good worker is all too conscious of how quickly the years are passing away, and bringing him nearer to the limit of his four-score years.

The delay of the printing-press has been the more tantalizing, inasmuch as four of the other Missions in Peking have now got printing-presses, and the English Church Mission and the Methodists each sent to ask Mr. Murray to send one of his men for a few days to teach them type-setting. "Happily," he says, "we have got a little start (with the old press), and our plan is unique—so are our compositors, the blind girls."

Not least among trials of patience must be reckoned the extraordinary difficulties which have attended the procuring of better premises, and which have compelled him, with his family and his blind pupils, to continue living in houses which several years ago were pronounced both insanitary and unsafe.

As a small instance of "hindering," I may mention that on hearing of the International Congress of Friends of the Blind, to be held at Chicago

Happily his friend Dr. T. Brown Henderson lost no time in starting a special collection for this beginning of WORK FOR THE ILLITERATE SIGHTED, and at last the metal types were cast, and were found to produce a printed page as clear as the finest copper engraving.

The first specimens reached Peking just ere the close of 1891. As soon as they arrived, Blind Peter and one of the blind girls were asked to feel them, and say if they knew what they were. They at once recognized them, and said, "This is our own type, but you have used lines instead of dots. Why have you done so?"

"BECAUSE YOU BLIND PEOPLE ARE NOW GOING TO PREPARE BOOKS FOR SIGHTED PERSONS, AND THEN YOU SHALL TEACH THEM HOW TO READ!"

And this is what is now being done. Surely a more pathetic turning of the tables was never devised!

Soon the first pages in the new type were printed, and proved beautifully clear and pleasant to the eye. Then came the anxiety as to whether the blind could teach the sighted to read from these pages. Great was the delight of both teachers and taught, when this was proved to be easily accomplished in a very brief period.

As Mr. Murray's special anxiety was to make this new art available for the poor converts, who are almost all utterly illiterate, one of his first cares was to select some of the dullest and oldest of these. But as ignorant persons in any country are not generally in haste to undertake new studies, however advantageous, it occurred to Mr. Murray to offer small rewards in cash to any elderly persons who

---

some years ago, I despatched to the care of the President of that Congress 500 copies of my little book on Murray's work, for gratuitous circulation. It appears that the Customs at Chicago made a claim for duty, and as I had not foreseen this, and requested him to pay it on my account, he did not care to do so, consequently the books were left at the Customs, and all subsequent efforts to reclaim them failed. We believe them to have been cremated, a suitable result of Satanic intervention to hinder the knowledge of Murray's work reaching so many persons specially interested in the Blind!

A page of the Epistle to the Romans in Mandarin Chinese in Murray's Numeral Type. Printed by the Blind in the School at Peking for Sighted persons.

would try to learn, and thus a class was formed of men and women, ranging from fifty-five to sixty-five years of age. He told them he wished them to try and learn to read, and when he added that he purposed giving each of them a sum equal to $2\frac{1}{2}d.$ a day while they were learning, they concluded that he had gone mad, but that it was a very pleasant form of madness, and they willingly agreed to come and be taught, and probably hoped this lavish provision would be continued to their lives' end. But, being Chinamen, they could not avoid a feeling of pride in attempting to acquire any literary skill, and to their own unbounded surprise and delight, they soon found they had succeeded, and at the end of six weeks they came to Mr. Murray to say they could no longer claim his daily $2\frac{1}{2}d.$, as they found that they all could not only read, but also write!

All this was most satisfactory; but as seeing is believing —*or at any rate is so to the unbiassed mind*—Mr. Murray invited a number of his brother missionaries and some other foreign residents to be present at a formal examination of a dozen other pupils, also taught by blind men and women. One of these had had his first lesson six days previously; he read without one mistake, though the examiners—the Rev. W. S. Ament, Rev. E. Bryant, Rev. J. Allardyce, and Professor S. M. Russell—purposely made him read words here and there in any part of the pages. The others likewise acquitted themselves to the entire satisfaction of all present—in fact they read better and more fluently than many Chinese students can do after several years of hard study of their own bewildering hieroglyphics.

Thus a good beginning was made, and ever since then, a certain number of blind compositors, chiefly girls, have been busy preparing pages in long columns from which, in the evenings, a sighted man prints off two hundred double sheets. Next morning the neat-fingered blind girls disperse and sort the type with perfect accuracy, and then prepare new pages for the printer. Thus in a few days some sacred Book is complete—a Gospel or an Epistle—and then the blind pupils fold and stitch it in its paper cover, and it is ready for sale to sighted readers. At first, should there be a demand for more than the two hundred copies, all had to be set up again, involving much waste of time and labour; but now the stereotype is employed, and an impression is kept of all books of Scripture, or hymns with or without their music.

Finding that multiplication of writing for the sighted, by his new system, was desirable, Murray set to work (always hampered by the difficulty of having only one arm to work with) to master letterpress printing and also lithography. He commenced work by making some cheap stones from which he succeeded in printing very fairly, when to his great joy a beautiful lithographic press arrived, which made his self-taught work a delight.

This, however, nowise lessens his anxiety to possess a first-class printing-press, with all the latest improvements, which shall enable him to print for the Chinese millions, when the supply has created the demand for his books. His own Committee have therefore decided to send him an excellent printing-press, so soon as the melting of the ice on the Pei Ho allows steamers to run to Tientsin.

Almost the very first to appreciate the latent value of this new invention were Mrs. Allardyce and her sister, Miss Goode—Australians. (The Rev. J. M. Allardyce is in charge of the West City station of the London Mission at Peking.) They are in the habit of every winter receiving a certain number of Christian women from distant farms, who, while work is slack, come to be taught, for a period of two to three months, during which they laboriously learn to read the Catechism and a few chapters of a Gospel in Chinese character. They then return home, able to read those only (as in any new chapter they would find ideographs which they had not learnt).

But in 1893, Mrs. Allardyce resolved to give the new system a trial, so she asked Mr. Murray whether he could prepare, in his new type, the Union Catechism, which is now used by all the Missions at Peking, and also some hymns and portions of Scripture, and WHETHER HE COULD SEND A BLIND GIRL TO TEACH THE CLASS?

Of course he was delighted. The blind compositors set to work, the pages were soon ready, including a selection of hymns with their tunes, the music being printed just in the same way as ordinary reading. Then Mrs. Murray took blind Ha Na (i.e. Hannah) in a native cart to the London Mission, and there left her alone with these Chinese women and the two foreign ladies as her pupils.

Within a week Mrs. Allardyce had mastered the system so thoroughly that she could puzzle it out for herself. (Of course she has a thorough knowledge of Chinese.) After a day or two more study one of the sighted women was able to write a letter quite clearly with all the tones perfectly indicated. (I have that letter now before me, as also a whole psalm written without a mistake by another woman, who had only been learning for a few days! I do not suppose that any of us could have done that a few days after we wrote our first stroke!)

I have also received a most pathetic photograph of this one blind girl surrounded by a dozen sighted women and eight children, whose presence must surely have added to the difficulties of both teacher and pupils!

Ere the end of the third month, all the farm women were able to read and write with enjoyment, and all had learnt to love their gentle, blind teacher. So thoroughly satisfied was Mrs. Allardyce with the success of this experiment, that she resolved that so soon as the farm workers returned to their homes she would commence a similar class for women living in the city.

Six months later Miss Goode visited these women at their villages, taking with her some newly printed hymns,

MUSICAL NOTES IN NUMERAL TYPE

one of which is here given with music—the Four Parts (each line contains two parts)—all exactly as written with the typewriter, which is used as for ordinary correspondence.

"THERE IS A FOUNTAIN FILLED WITH BLOOD."—*Cowper.*

This, with portions of Scripture, they read at sight,

or if they found any symbol which they did not at once recognize, they "reckoned" it (just as we should spell a doubtful word) and then rendered it, and the tones, quite correctly. They read right through the Gospel of St. Mark with the greatest interest and pleasure. Well may Mr. Murray, in relating this, add, "You will be able to see the importance of this change to the little Church, and to the women themselves."

Other women in these villages were so astonished and delighted at the literary skill of their friends, that a very large number entered their names as anxious to be taught in the following winter, but ere that season came, the war with Japan had broken out, and as all Mission work was necessarily stopped for a season, Mrs. Allardyce and her sister profited by this opportunity to visit their father in Australia. While there they were greatly cheered by the receipt of several clear, well-written letters in Numeral-Type from the farm women who had come to them the previous winter so utterly ignorant, and who could now easily accomplish a feat which comparatively few of their countrymen can do, namely, that of writing a simple letter to a friend. Of course they had to get some literary friend to address their envelopes.

The great satisfaction of having thus proved how easy the new method is to poor, illiterate peasants, lies in the fact that these form the enormous majority of the converts of all Christian Missions in China. Mr. Murray says: "All the women and ninety-five per cent. of the men are illiterate." Now, as in the days of old, it may be asked, "Have any of the Rulers of the people believed?" And the reply will still be, "To the poor the Gospel is preached." Whatever they learn is acquired orally. In church they can join only in such hymns as they have learnt by heart—and in the same way they can only carry home such verses of the Bible or of hymns as they have thus learnt. So it is no small matter to have discovered a simple method by which these can carry the Word of Life into their own homes, there to study it for themselves and to impart it to others.

Here, then, we have the history of the early infancy of a great work. Like other healthy plants, this baby-tree has been quietly growing up from its obscure cradle beneath the soil, destined, I firmly believe, to become a wide-spreading Tree of Life—a mighty agent in the extension of that kingdom which cometh not with observation. I believe that what the invention of alphabetic printing has proved to the whole civilized world, except China, Murray's Numeral Type will eventually become to all Christian Missions throughout at least four-fifths of the vast Chinese Empire. He has already proved that in its adaptation to the use of the blind, it is as clearly understood by people of the far south and north as by those of the extreme east and west.

Among the pupils who have come to his school for the blind, there have been men from Manchuria, Chih-li, Shan-si, Shantung, Hupeh, and Kuantung—that is to say, from the extreme north-east of the Empire to the far south; and though their pronunciation differed so greatly that some could scarcely understand one another, all alike read from the same Scripture; and all who have mastered the system are confident that it will be found equally applicable to every part of China where Mandarin dialects are spoken.

If this is the case with the blind, how much more certain is it that the identical system can be read by the sighted persons of all these provinces?

And this brings us to the grand point, namely, that the natural inference is that ONE VERSION OF THE HOLY SCRIPTURES, PRINTED IN THE NUMERAL TYPE, WILL BE CURRENT THROUGHOUT THE MANDARIN PROVINCES, because, being read by numbers, not phonetically, the varied pronunciation of different dialects is of no consequence. Each symbol represents the sound as uttered by the people of any district. Just as in Scotland the word *over* is sometimes rendered *o'wer* (pronounced *hour*), and in poetry becomes *o'er*, so words which at Peking are pronounced K'uo and Yung, are pronounced K'o and Jung fifty miles to the south. We know that in our own little island, peasants from Somerset, York, Glasgow or Aberdeen, while reading from the same book as a London "cockney," will each pronounce it very differently from the cultured man of letters. But in Great China many different versions would be absolutely necessary, even in Mandarin-speaking Provinces, were the Roman Alphabet employed, whereas by Mr. Murray's system each reader will recognize the numeral, and pronounce it his own way.

As an example of this varied pronunciation I may mention how even so excellent a Chinese scholar as the late Dr. Williamson, coming to Peking from the next Province in Mr. Murray's absence, bade his servant go and buy five catties of Niu Jow, but pronounced it Yoo, so instead of a good piece of beef, the man brought a large lump of suet, which was strictly correct, but very trying to a hungry man.

Sir Harry Parkes told me how he had once ordered, for Lord Elgin, a large supply of (I think) potatoes, and after a most irritating delay, received a huge consignment of crabs!

The difference between many of the Chinese dialects is so great that the people of different Provinces literally cannot understand one another's speech. Those who can read and write have recourse to slates and write their conversation. Others who have acquired the atrocious *patois* called Pigeon (or Business) English, talk that.

In view of the fact that the enormous majority of Christian converts are of the poor classes, who would never attempt a task so difficult as that of learning to read and write their own bewildering character, it was an immense

ADVANTAGES OF NUMERAL TYPE

gain when it was found possible to prepare versions of the Bible in our own Roman letters, not only in pure Mandarin Chinese, but also in the local dialects of several districts. By this means the native Christians of these favoured localities have been enabled to learn to read with comparative facility, writing being of course a separate study.

But to the Chinese mind an alphabetic system is so essentially foreign as to be inherently repugnant. Herein the Murray Numeral Type possesses an initial advantage, its simple, angular symbols being attractive to the people, and easily written on Chinese paper with the tiny brush and paint which are the Chinese equivalents of pen and ink.* Moreover, several persons who have mastered both the Roman and the Murray, or Numeral Type, affirm that the latter is very much easier, to say nothing of the advantage of SIMULTANEOUSLY ACQUIRING THE POWER OF READING AND WRITING.

The Murray type has also an immense advantage in regard to speed. Suppose a test-trial between two persons of equal ability, either in type-writing or with the pen; the writer in Murray type will produce nearly 400 words, while his competitor produces 100 alphabetically, and moreover saves two-thirds of his paper—a detail which not only implies economy of material, but great convenience in storage, and facility in the carriage of a large number of books.

Another very important point is that in the new type most of the work is done by the blind students in school, all correcting of proofs is done on the spot, and THE COST OF A COMPLETE BIBLE, WITH THE "TONES" AND ASPIRATE OF EVERY WORD PERFECTLY RENDERED, WILL BE ABOUT

---

* By a curious misnomer we call their paint "Indian ink," whereas it is all manufactured in China, chiefly in the Province of Wuhu. It is a most elaborate process, and varies greatly in quality, its price ranging from less than 2s. to 7l. per pound (i.e. about thirty-two of the pieces in ordinary use). Gold-leaf, to impart a metallic lustre, and musk, of the musk-rat, to scent it, are among the costly ingredients.

ONE-THIRD THAT OF A SIMILAR BOOK PRODUCED ALPHA-
BETICALLY BY SPECIALLY-TRAINED SIGHTED COMPOSITORS
AND PROOF-READERS.

Mr. Murray considers that it is now fully proved that the new type is not only the easiest conceivable form to read and write, but that it is by far the cheapest to produce, and must necessarily make the smallest possible book.

BEST OF ALL, IT PROMISES A SOLUTION OF ONE OF HIS GRAVEST PROBLEMS, IN THE PROVISION OF ALMOST INEXHAUSTIBLE STORES OF REMUNERATIVE OCCUPATION FOR THE BLIND, AS COMPOSITORS, PRINTERS, BINDERS AND TEACHERS.

He has done his best to teach them certain trades, and has found his pupils very successful in making door-mats and coarse matting for passages, while the women learn knitting and sewing mattresses and pillows. Various other work has been tried, such as shoe-making (the Chinese cloth shoe resembling a shapeless boat !) The latter, however, has not proved successful.

And, indeed, as regards making them self-supporting by instruction in any of the usual industrial arts, Mr. Murray despairs of the blind ever being able to compete against the legions of sighted Chinese who already overcrowd the market for basket and cane work, knitting, weaving, &c., and who would inevitably undersell the produce of the blind. He says : " The Christian Church here is a mere handful of outcasts surrounded by hordes of unfriendly heathen. Where is the sympathy to encourage teaching the blind any handicraft ? Even in England, what would become of their industries apart from hearts in sympathy and open purses to help ? "

So it appears that embossing, stereotyping, and bookbinding, piano and harmonium tuning and teaching, knitting and mat-making, are the most promising industries of the class usually considered suitable for the blind, and that their employment must lie chiefly in literary and musical work. They also write out books of embossed manuscript music, which they stitch and bind very decently. Ever on the alert to turn their musical instincts to account, Mr. Murray is now teaching them to construct dulcimers, for which he believes a demand may be created, and that some will find employment in teaching sighted persons to play these as an accompaniment to sacred lyrics.

This first step in the manufacture of musical instruments has awakened a larger ambition. An old harmonium having recently come to grief, he took it to pieces, and with the aid of his pupils, he assorted a new set of tuneful reeds, with such satisfactory result that now he has half-developed plans for getting a Chinese carpenter to construct rude wooden cases, within which the blind pupils may arrange reeds, &c., and so produce instruments which may at least do for teaching those pupils whom they hope to attract from middle-class or even upper families.

A friend, who had seen how many blind men in Japan earn their living by massage, suggested that Mr. Murray should introduce this as a profession, but he finds that the Chinese do not use it, at least not in North China.

The same friend had suggested teaching the blind telegraphy, and was interested to learn that it had been one of Mr. Murray's early ideas. He says: "Between our front and back courts I had overhead wires laid. And in a cupboard in each room I had two electric bells of different tones. By having the connections cut, each bell gave only a single stroke for one touch of the key, so that with but few signs, it was like a voice speaking! Having our 'code' fixed (it was of course our own plan of lessons), we held intercourse, and in that way communicated music lessons. When a boy came from the back room and read his piece of music, and found it correct, what pleasure it gave him! He was like a child with a new toy! In 1886, I had to prepare to return to Scotland, and the telegraphy was put aside. Since my return to China, I have not been able to take the matter up, but I have all the material here, and might easily have the thing started again."

(In the meanwhile the Chinese have themselves organized a telegraphic code, telegraphing only numerals, which indicate the 6000 hieroglyphics in most common use.)

Though there seems so little hope of the students in the Blind School becoming self-supporting by ordinary industries, they are unwearied in their exertions on behalf of their sighted brothers and sisters.

It is truly said that a bad workman quarrels with his tools, but in Mr. Murray's hands all tools and all materials are turned to good account. Here is his account of how his blind pupils prepared the first hymn-book for sighted singers : " The book, which will consist of about 150 pages, is in size about four by five inches, and half an inch thick. We have still twenty hymns to do, but the stencils are used up. I have some old ones which I bought in Glasgow, and although damaged, I think they will do. But even with them, I do not know if we will have enough." (And if not, then what a weary time of waiting ere more could be procured, and the book so eagerly desired, be finished.)

It next occurred to him to print the lessons for the sighted in very large letters on wall-sheets. He divided the space into squares, and got a native engraver to cut each symbol. From these, moulds were taken, and then each was stereotyped on a separate plate, and from these he can now print very effective sheets, which can be mounted on cloth for the use of classes.

Writing in 1894, Mr. Murray thus describes his hive of busy blind bees at their work : " With the exception of two, who are making rope door-mats, two boys who are at the Braille stereotype, making the brass sheets from which the embossing is done for blind readers, and some who are re-tuning the piano, all hands are busy preparing books for sighted readers ; boys or girls are composing and distributing ; the Chinese scholar is reading proof-sheets ;

one man is preparing the papier-mâché with which to take a mould; another is boiling the metal to pour on to other moulds; two men are at the press, printing the Gospels; two are in the shop, printing the London Mission Hymnal.

"Two girls at a time work part of each day as compositors. They work in this way: the first girl reads with one hand on her Gospel in raised type for the blind, while with the other hand she lifts the two types representing each word in the type for the sighted, and hands them to the second girl to place in the form for printing. Thus the two blind girls work till a paragraph is finished. Then the second girl reads from the type thus set up (of course it is all reversed, but to the blind this is just as easy to read, as their every-day writing with punctured dots is all written backward, and when taken off the frame has to be turned over, and then is right for the reader). While one girl reads, the other follows with her finger on the Gospel in the raised Braille Type, and so checks any mistake.

"In this way we have set up and printed 100 copies of smaller Epistles; 400 copies of the Gospel of St. Matthew; 400 copies of St. Mark; 400 copies of St. Luke; 1200 copies of St. John as far as the 10th chapter; 1400 sheets of reading exercises; 100 hymn-books, all for the use of sighted persons, and now ready for distribution as the demand arises.

"We have had the 408 sounds of the syllabary arranged according to our primer, and lithographed, making four pages in large type of about half an inch in size. These are stitched in the form of a book, and are supplied to beginners. A large number of these are now in use, and I have sent many to missionary friends who wished to study the lessons. So our school this year has been like a wholesale publishing house. And if all could see the joy which lights up the blind faces to find themselves thus useful and important, I think that from the Emperor downward all would give us their sympathy and help. All the pupils have had a trial as compositors, distributors, and proof-readers, each has had a sighted pupil to teach, and all feel the utmost confidence in their prospects of success as teachers. This indeed has already been SO AMPLY PROVED that ALL THEORETICAL OBJECTIONS should now be silenced."

It was by this time fully proven that the Numeral Type is wonderfully simple and intelligible to the Chinese, whether blind or sighted ; but to the great majority of foreigners it was perplexing till Professor S. M. Russell, M.A.,* of the Imperial College at Peking, wrote a very detailed explanation of the system in English, with tables illustrating the whole so clearly that none acquainted with Chinese could fail to understand them.

When complete there was some difficulty in getting it printed. At the printing press of the American Board of Missions there was no foreign superintendent, and the only Chinaman who could set up English was called away on Government duty. In this dilemma Mr. Murray sought the aid of the Roman Catholic fathers in the West City. Their English being as imperfect as Mr. Murray's French, they all talked Chinese, and agreed to do the work, Mr. Murray himself correcting the English proofs, and one of the pupils going daily to set up the illustration of the Numeral Type.

A slight difficulty arose in regard to printing the final illustration, which was to have been the Lord's Prayer, but as the Protestant translation differs slightly from that used by the Roman Catholics, Mr. Murray agreed to change this to the native Chinese "Three Character Classic," and so that difficulty was obviated, and the pamphlet most satisfactorily completed. Of the 1200 copies printed, about 200 had been sent to persons likely to be interested, when the progress of the war with Japan stopped this and other work. Mr. Murray left about fifty copies at the Shanghai Mission

---

* Of whom Murray writes : " He is a staunch friend—he befriended us when we were most in need."

Press with a request that they might be advertised as being there for sale, so that persons interested might order copies.

A reprint of it will be found at the end of this book.

At first it was hoped that the war would be confined to Korea, but as the summer wore on it became evident that the invading forces of Japan were bent on shaking the very foundations of the Manchu Empire, and as operations began to close towards Peking, and the streets of the capital itself were thronged with hordes of undisciplined Chinese troops from country districts, far more dangerous to foreigners than the Japanese invaders, very grave alarm was felt.

On the 4th October, a circular was issued by the British Minister of Legation, requiring all foreign women and children to leave Peking within two days. This sudden necessity for flight was especially trying to Mrs. Murray, with her five children ranging from seven years to fourteen days old. Happily her husband was entitled to his year's furlough, so he was able to decide that instead of living at great expense at Shanghai (which was already thronged with refugees), he would escort his family direct to Scotland.

Then followed two days of tremendous effort and work, in which his one arm had to do the work of ten, in packing and sorting household and school goods. He sent as many of his pupils as had available homes, to their own people, and left the others in charge of several gentlemen of the Local Committee, who proposed remaining on the field to look after their people, and who promised to keep work going on at the Blind School, each undertaking to visit it on certain definite days.

Then the Mission House (dilapidated as it was!) had to be put in order, books and furniture left as secure as circumstances admitted of, the family packing accomplished, and commissariat arrangements made for the journey. By the kindness of a friend, who lent Mrs. Murray a chair carried by coolies, they were enabled to avoid the Peiho river, and to travel by land to Tientsin, whence steamers ply to Shanghai.

At Tientsin there was a delay of four days, during which Mr. Murray was gladdened by much hearty sympathy evinced towards his work, several missionaries pledging themselves to make the teaching of the illiterate by the blind a primary object in opening up new country districts. A lady, who was likewise detained for some days at Tientsin, turned that delay to excellent account in teaching the art of reading in Numeral Type for the sighted, to a native Bible woman from another district, and so well did her pupil prosper that ere they parted, each to her native country, the lady was able to give the Bible woman a certificate of qualification, showing that she was competent to teach other women in her far-away district. So the work spreads as opportunity offers, and this exemplifies how it may gradually cover the great Empire.

On arriving at Shanghai, "the great Athens of China," Mr. Murray found that he had three days to wait ere the steamer would sail for London, and these days also he was able to turn to account The recent publication in *The Messenger* of the very favourable review of Professor S. M. Russell's pamphlet, "Explanation of Mr. Murray's System of Teaching the Sighted," had called attention to this further development of his work, and he was cordially welcomed and much encouraged by several leading missionaries. Not least satisfactory was a letter from the learned Dr. Fryer, translator and publisher of scientific works in Chinese, who, being surrounded by military cordons, could not arrange a personal interview, but wrote: "Let me tell you that I am using your method for the Shanghai dialect on my typewriter." That surely is conclusive evidence in its favour, the more so as the dialect spoken at Shanghai is non-Mandarin.

The homeward journey to London, and thence to Glasgow, was uneventful, though the care of five babies who could

Photo by Ovinius Davis, Edinburgh

THE REV. W. H. MURRAY'S FOUR ELDEST CHILDREN.

not speak a word of English—only pure Mandarin Chinese—was no trifle to the anxious parents, who were thankful indeed to find themselves safe in Scotland. Their too brief stay was anything but restful, as there was much to do, and they were resolved to return early in October, so as to reach Peking ere the freezing of the Peiho cut off the capital from communication with the outer world.

Of course their first care on their return was to re-assemble the scattered students, and once again to make the best of the dilapidated old Chinese houses which had been condemned as dangerous six years previously, but which were still the Mission premises. It was found that in consequence of the war, all prices had risen so much that the money previously collected for re-building was insufficient, so a further delay arose till more could be collected.

Meanwhile 1896 brought the first domestic sorrow to the little home. The new year brought a sixth addition to the family—a beautiful blue-eyed baby. But the care of five young children, without any attendant to help her on the long return journey to Peking, had seriously affected the mother's health, and she was unable to give him the same devoted personal care as the others had enjoyed.

When the summer heat and rains drew near, the Doctor insisted that they must all leave the city and find healthier quarters in the hills, so they found lodgings in a temple, two hundred years old, picturesquely situated between two mountain torrents and overshadowed by fine old trees. This temple is the private property of two brothers of the blood royal, who lock up the idols and pay no attention to them, and who were most kind to the Murrays, allowing them to lodge at a very low rent.

All profited by the change except the beautiful and singularly wise and winsome baby, whose large wondering blue eyes seemed to appeal so pathetically for comfort in his constant suffering. Not all the care of two kind doctors could save the little life, and on Friday night, the 10th July,

NOTE TO PAGE III.

It may cheer some (who being held prisoner by pain and weakness, are tempted to deem themselves cut off from active work) to trace the history of this generous gift back to its source.

The steamer in which a Blind Lady and her friend were travelling touched at a town in New Zealand, where the friend landed to visit a lady who was quite confined to her bed. This lady lent her the story of Mr. Murray's life and work to read to her blind friend, whose interest was thus so effectually aroused that she procured other copies of the book to lend to other people.

Amongst those to whom she told the story was a lady who soon afterwards returned to England, and by her timely guarantee of £1000 so cheered other workers, that the necessary sum for better premises was secured. The guarantee was then taken up by the Father of the Blind Lady. But the first thread in this web of very practical interest was spun in that quiet sick-room.

little Matthew ended his brief experience of earthly trials, leaving very sore hearts mourning for him. The little coffin arrived at 1 a.m. on Sunday morning. At 3 a.m. several friends came from the hill sanatorium of the London Mission, and (some on ponies, some on donkeys) accompanied the sorrowing parents to the cemetery outside the city walls on the south-west side, where they were met by other friends bringing flowers and a lovely wreath. Even the donkey boys gathered lovely large white convolvuli to lay on the little coffin which was carried by four Chinamen. Four more carried the mother in a covered chair. Heavy rain-clouds threatened a down-pour all day, but happily the storm was stayed till towards evening, when all had got safely back to the hills.

The enforced delay in regard to rebuilding the Mission house proved a blessing in disguise. Mr. Murray had all along urged that instead of rebuilding on the same cramped site, which would necessitate making the house two stories high—a detail very seriously objected to by the Chinese for superstitious reasons—we should endeavour to raise a sum sufficient to secure a larger property which would allow space for the extension of the Blind School and development of the Printing Works, instead of everything being overcrowded with no room whatever for expansion.

Subscriptions for even the minor outlay had however come in so slowly, that this larger hope was not seriously entertained till the summer of 1896, when a letter was received from a lady offering to guarantee £1000 of the whole cost, provided that steps were at once taken to make up the previously collected building fund to a similar sum by Christmas, 1896.

This generous offer cheered the somewhat disheartened collectors, who set to work with renewed vigour, and succeeded in raising the required sum. The lady's action evoked the sympathy of a friend in New Zealand, who in the name of his own blind daughter, paid the £1000 she had guaranteed, so we naturally supposed there would be no further delay, and that in a very short time the Murray family and all the blind pupils would be safely established in one of several desirable properties known to be for sale, and having on them ready-built Chinese houses, which could easily be adapted to the requirements of the Mission. But we forgot that we had to reckon with Chinese prejudices!

In order to waste no time, our Committee in Peking had commenced their investigations for suitable premises, as soon as they heard of the aforesaid guarantee, and from that time till the following summer (July, 1897) the leading members were by turns engaged in negotiating for sundry desirable properties, always to find themselves thwarted, and that the negotiations had to be broken off. The fact is that any respectable Chinaman can scarcely bring himself to face the disgrace of selling land to a foreigner. He would sell to an insignificant Chinaman, who might in his turn sell to us. But this might involve risk of finding the title deeds insecure, and that is a very important matter.

Moreover every transaction of any importance in China, is done by Go-Betweens, whether it is arranging a marriage between the son of one man with the daughter of another, or the purchase of a neighbour's house, all has to be arranged in this circuitous manner. The principals never meet, so neither really knows the true mind of the other, nor to what extent the Go-Betweens are each trying to feather their own nests.

The result in this case has been that with money in hand for the purchase of apparently ideal premises which are standing waiting for a purchaser, the poor Murrays and their blind scholars have had to endure yet another rainy season in the dangerous and unwholesome houses which were condemned fully six years ago, and again all have suffered more or less from malaria and other evil consequences of their insanitary surroundings. Truly those who devote their lives to working in China for the good of their fellow creatures, have special need of God-given patience.

And this they seem to have acquired to a remarkable degree (doubtless long practice makes perfect), for it is we in Britain who have waxed impatient, and the sufferers on the spot have reminded us that "We must wait till God opens the way; to attempt to do otherwise would mean miserable failure. Under His direct management His people took over forty years to travel a journey which a caravan could travel in three or four days." And again, "People at home can have no conception of what it is to do such a thing in China. Some of the Missions have spent as much as seven years in negotiating the purchase of suitable land."

At last their patience has been rewarded, and an excellent property has been secured in the West City, close to the London Mission, where Mr. and Mrs. Allardyce and Miss Goode have already proved themselves such appreciative helpers.

All previous efforts had been directed to secure premises in the East City, in the neighbourhood of the present school, which has the advantage for Mr. and Mrs. Murray and their family, of being near the place where the Union Service in English is held every Sunday evening. Of course this weekly meeting with fellow countrymen and women is a very cheering incident to the foreigners resident in the heart of the great city so "wholly given to idolatry."

But in all other respects the advantages are on the side of the newly acquired property. To begin with, the East City is largely composed of squalid, narrow streets, all densely peopled, whereas the West City has wide open spaces and a far less crowded population. The new premises occupy a nice healthy position on high ground near one of the city gates, and consequently near the open country. The medical attendant of the Mission looks confidently for a marked improvement in the health of all concerned, European and Chinese. On this site stand several good old Chinese bungalows (i.e. one-storied houses with verandah) which, although out of repair, are all built of such excellent material, that by partial repairing and some rebuilding, a satisfactory Mission Station will be provided, with large schools for blind lads and blind women, a good dwelling house for the Murrays, a workshop, a house for printing office, a book-room for the Bible Society's books, and ample space for extension when the work is further developed.

At present all the buildings rise like so many islands from a sea of rank weeds, but all will soon be made tidy. Among the chief advantages of the property is the fact that it possesses a well of good water—an item of the utmost importance.

The credit of conducting all the delicate negotiations for this purchase, and bringing them to a successful issue, is due to the Rev. S. E. Meech of the London Mission.

An equally good property in the East City would have been much more costly, for, as in China all things seem to go contrary to the rest of the world, the East City has hitherto been the fashionable end; but now that a railway has actually been opened between Peking and its port at Tientsin and that trains are daily running to the terminus (which is in the country, about two miles from the South-West gate of the Chinese City),* it seems inevitable that the hitherto sleepy West City will awaken, and that it will become the most important quarter, perhaps even as in London, Glasgow, and other cities in the old world, the West End will become the fashionable end. Certainly it must prove an advantage to the Mission Station to be several miles nearer to the railway terminus, especially

* For superstitious reasons, incomprehensible to any but a Chinaman, the railway is not allowed to come within about two miles of the City walls. The marvel is that it has been allowed at all.

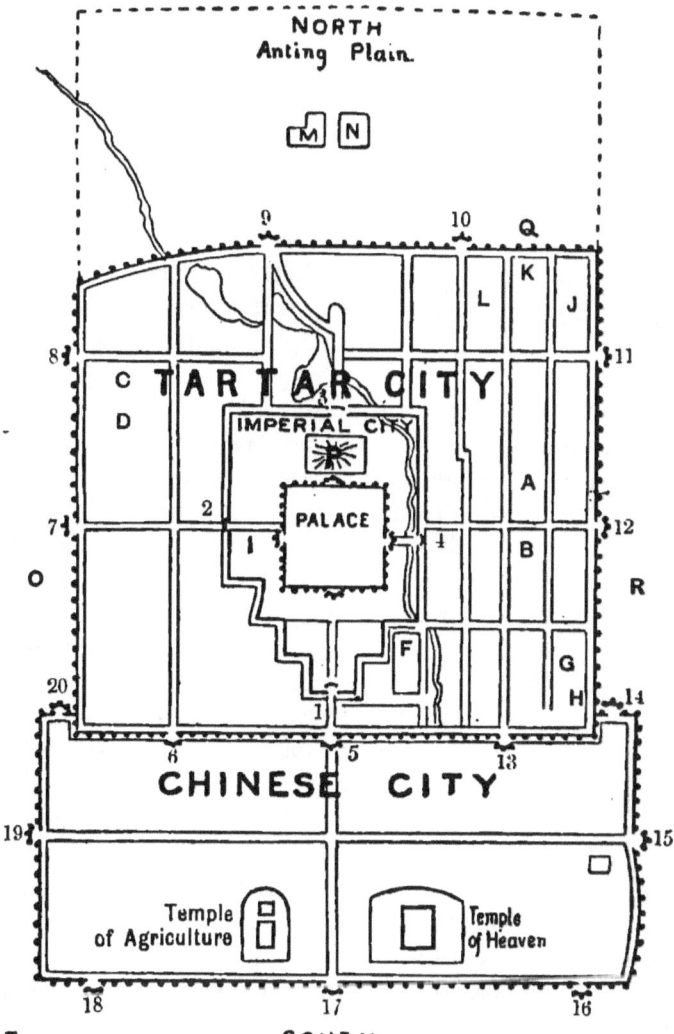

PLAN OF PEKING. By WILLIAM SIMPSON, F.R.G.S.

1 to 4. The Four Gates of the Imperial City.
5 to 13. The Nine Gates of the Tartar City.
14 to 20. The Seven Gates of the Chinese City.
A. Site of the present School for the Blind.
B. London Society's Mission, East.
C. London Society's Mission, West.
D. Site of the new School for the Blind.
E. Terminus of Railway from the Port of Tientsin, hereabouts.
F. Foreign Legations.
G. Examination Hall.
H. Observatory.
I. Pehtang. French Ecclesiastical Mission.
J. Russian Mission.
K. Tung Ho-Kung. Lama Temple.
L. Confucian Temple and Hall of the Classics.
M and N. Lama Temples.
O. Altar to the Moon.
P. Mei Shan. Artificial hill made of coal.
Q. Altar to the Earth.
R. Altar to the Sun.

when heavy parcels of books have to be despatched from the printing press at Peking to distant Provinces. Mr. Murray, writing in July, says: "It takes such a time to plod through mud in broiling heat, from the Blind School in the East City, to the London Mission" in the West.

I should mention that the terms East and West City refer to the two sides of the Tartar or Manchu City. A glance at the accompanying map will show how remarkable a feature of this great northern capital of the Chinese Empire, is its division into distinct cities, each separated from the others by great castellated walls. These seem like the work of giants, and they are entered by massive gateways, each of which is closed at sunset, and the key delivered up to high officials, so that it is truly a serious matter to find oneself at night on the wrong side of a wall!

The city of the conquering Tartars lies to the north—it is a great walled square. The Chinese city is an oblong, lying to the south, the south wall of the Tartar city forming its north wall. In the centre of the Tartar city another walled square is the Imperial city, in the heart of which (as a precious gem enclosed in successive caskets) another walled square encloses the grounds of the Imperial Palace, within whose sacred precincts no foreign barbarian has ever been suffered to set foot. Of these beautiful Imperial pleasure-grounds, however, some glimpses may be obtained from certain points in the Imperial city—looking across the great moat, especially from a noble nine-arched white marble bridge, six hundred feet in length, which spans a very pretty artificial lake on whose clear waters float lovely water lilies and lotus blossoms.

Under Mr. Murray's kind escort, I found myself there one morning at the first glimmer of dawn, looking across a cool green meadow, shaded by weeping willows, to the park-like foliage, from which rise many attractive curved roofs of brilliant apple-green or golden-yellow tiles, dazzlingly bright in the light of the morning sun. At the further end of the lake lie the various buildings of the palace. I could see one with high triple-roof surrounded by a whole cluster of fanciful double-roofed buildings, while a little further lies another great yellow-roofed palace. Just within the wall on that side is a very fine Imperial Temple, or rather group of temples, with many gables and most complicated triple roofs, all yellow of course being Imperial, and this is approached by three wondrously gorgeous triple " pai-lows " (commemorative gateways) all of dazzling yellow china. These temples are faced with china of the most elaborate patterns, in which of course the dragon and phœnix figure largely.*

To return from these picturesque details to the educational subject. Of course Murray's system has not escaped a certain amount of that adverse criticism which seems to be the fate of every invention for the true good of mankind. His reply is characteristic. " Blind Bartimeus was not to be so easily silenced! May he be our example, and may we succeed as well." " If the Enemy prevailed, there could be no united action. EVERY DISTRICT THROUGHOUT CHINA WOULD REQUIRE TO HAVE ITS OWN PECULIAR VERSION. There could be no central depot."

A recent writer on the best method by which to represent Chinese sounds in all the varied dialects of China, rather set aside the Numeral Type, on the ground that it was still in its infancy. So it is. In its application to sighted persons, it has only been in type about five years. Four hundred and fifty years ago, exactly the same objection might have been raised to the art of printing, as now practised throughout all the civilized world except China. Our hope is that long ere one century has passed, very many thousands of Chinese men and women will by means of this system be able to read the Holy Scriptures for themselves, and to teach their children to do so.

* For fuller details of Peking and its Temples, see " Wanderings in China." By C. F. Gordon-Cumming. Published by Blackwood.

From time to time encouragements reach Mr. Murray in the form of letters from missionaries in distant Provinces, who have procured copies of his primers for both blind and sighted persons, and who have not only puzzled them out for themselves, but have then instructed blind persons, who in their turn have taught others.

So AT LAST we hope that his long years of patience are about to be rewarded by his being allowed to "see of the travail of his soul," for truly he has travailed, working ceaselessly to the utmost limit of human endurance, in a climate where the most stifling summer heat combines with pitiless rains to produce pestilential miasma and all the evils born of malaria, while in winter the cold is so intense that for many months the river is frozen.

In such a climate the mere work of a colporteur involves great physical strain, but in Mr. Murray's case, the additional long hours which for so many years have been stolen from sleep for the study (often by very defective lamplight) of the most intricate characters, beginning with Greek and Hebrew, and now for twenty-six years or bewildering Chinese—all combined with very extensive correspondence—have sorely overstrained his precious eyesight, and caused him many an anxious qualm. So it is time he had his reward, in proving that his system is now so clearly worked out, that other men can take it up and make use of it, simply from the study of his Primers.

♪ Happily a considerable number of missionaries, especially in North China, are now waking up to understand the value of his inventions, and all those who have really tried them are enthusiastic, and describe them as a Heaven-revealed blessing for the good of the illiterate sighted, as well as for the blind. Others are quite willing to send blind converts to Peking to be trained and then start schools in their own Province, if only their Home Societies will authorize the initial expenses.

On this subject Mr. Murray writes: "MONEY IS THE

OBSTACLE IN EVERY CASE. Missionaries themselves have not the means to spare, and as yet the Missions have no appropriation for teaching their people to read. If we had some Apostle at home, just to show to the Societies the importance of this matter, no doubt the money would be voted and the work of the Missions would increase with a bound. The work of each man in the field would equal that of ten now."

As yet only five schools have been commenced at different Mission stations, in five of the Mandarin-speaking Provinces, the teachers having in each case been sent to the parent school in Peking to be trained. It is hoped that from these small seed-plots others will develop, and also that all the principal Christian Missions may send agents — either Europeans, or carefully selected Chinese converts—to be trained by Mr. Murray, that they may carry his system to every existing Mission Station. It is very desirable that in the first instance, as many as possible should be brought under his own strong personal influence. Then one such SIGHTED head-teacher in each district could there found a Blind School, and train Chinese Scripture Readers, and thus the work may be ceaselessly extended in every direction, till it overspreads the whole vast Empire like a network of fertilizing streams from the River of the Water of Life.

That it is already thus extending is certain—slowly and not "with observation," yet surely, and in a manner which leaves no room for doubt of widespread results in the near future.

I am tempted to recall a hopeful analogy from the natural world. When I was travelling in the Pacific, I stayed awhile off the coast of New Zealand on the little Isle of Kawau, long the home of Sir George Grey, who loved thereon to acclimatize all manner of plants and living creatures from other countries. One day the captain of a trading vessel brought him a pair of lovely little tree-kangaroos, pretty furry creatures about the size of a hare which climb trees like squirrels. These were turned loose in the woods, and for several years were no more seen. It was feared that they were dead, when, to Sir George's delight, he one day observed a pair playing on the grass. Soon another and another were seen, and ere long they were found to have multiplied and overspread the Isle to such an extent, that at the time of my visit they were almost as numerous as rabbits in Scotland.

So we may hope that the humble readers who have returned from Peking to their own villages are even now, all alone in their own homes, teaching many of their friends, who in their turn will teach others, and thus silently the good leaven will spread.

We have to remember that in China everything moves very slowly, and that NOTHING IS SO OBNOXIOUS AS NOVELTY, WHICH ASSUREDLY IS A STRIKING FEATURE IN ALL THIS WORK. Happily it is commended to the people of Peking by the fact of Mr. Murray's having been continually amongst them for a quarter of a century of friendly intercourse. His kindly and genial manners, and inexhaustible patience, have gained their confidence in a remarkable degree, and have predisposed them to receive his innovations with less suspicion than would meet those of a new comer.

This New Mission will certainly appeal, as no other has yet done, to two of the strongest characteristics of China's millions, namely, *their reverence for pure benevolence, and their veneration for the power of reading.* To see foreigners undertaking such a work of love for the destitute blind, and for those who, though endowed with sight, are utterly illiterate, will go far towards dispelling prejudice against Christians and their MASTER, and will prepare the way for the workers of all Christian Missions.

I would earnestly entreat all who have already helped it, not to allow their interest in the subject to flag, but on the contrary, to do all in their power to awaken that of others. For though I am fully convinced that this Agency is destined to do a very great work in China, it is as yet only a Baby-Giant, and stands greatly in need of the care of as many foster-mothers as possible—(in the way of collectors).

Assuredly no Mission-field is more certain ere long to yield fruit an hundred-fold than this Chinese Empire; and I know of no Agency which is more surely destined to work among the masses, as an ever-spreading leaven of all good, than this training of Scripture Readers, who year by year may be sent forth from this school to read the Sacred Message in the streets of Peking and other great centres of heathenism, holding forth to others the LIGHT which has gladdened their own lives.

SURELY SUCH A STORY AS THIS MAY WELL INCITE MANY TO PROVE THEIR INTEREST BY SOME ACT OF SELF-DENIAL, WHICH MAY ENABLE THEM TO HELP SO EARNEST A WORKER. (For we all know how very apt we are to limit our giving-power to such a sum as we can spare without involving much self-denial!)

Would that some who read these lines would consider for a moment what life would be to themselves were they deprived of gifts so precious as SIGHT and LIGHT, and would each resolve to present for this branch of GOD's work such a sum as he shall really miss—not taken from the total of his accustomed offerings, but as a Special Thank-offering for these precious gifts—a portion of that money-talent which we know we only hold in trust, as we so often need to remind ourselves when we say, " Both riches and honour come of THEE, and of THINE own do we give THEE."

LETTERS FROM COMPETENT WITNESSES.

IN conclusion, I may quote a few of the many testimonies we have received from men of experience in Chinese matters, who have seen for themselves the practical results of the work.

In May, 1890, a great Missionary Conference was held at Shanghai, and as by this time several other systems had been devised for teaching the blind, chiefly in the Southern Provinces, this was one of the subjects to be considered. It was therefore deemed desirable that Mr. Murray should attend the Conference.

He accordingly went to Shanghai, accompanied by Blind Peter, and read a descriptive paper, which, however lucid to Chinese hearers, seems to have somewhat perplexed his European audience. But when Peter's turn came to give practical illustrations of reading, writing, and playing the church organ, his reception was enthusiastic. Several Missionaries from Peking who were present, testified from personal knowledge to the like ability of other boys and men, girls and women, in the Blind School. Even the President left the chair that he might tell how, when he was in Peking, he had sung a tune to one of Mr. Murray's pupils—a tune which probably no one in Peking had ever heard before—and how the blind man had noted it down by his system, and in a very few moments reproduced it perfectly on the harmonium.

Mr. Murray very unfortunately assumed that he had now done all that was required to secure support, and, being anxious to catch the return steamer to Peking, he forthwith departed, without waiting to take part in the deliberations of the small Committee which was subsequently appointed by the Conference to consider which of the various systems that within the last few years have been evolved for the use of the blind, should be adopted throughout China.

The supporters of several other systems were on the Committee, and the truth of the old proverb, "The absent are always in the wrong," was once more proved, for, to the amazement of all who understood the practical working of Murray's system, it was simply ignored, and a statement was widely circulated to the effect that it was not taken into consideration, not being considered sufficiently simple!

Thereupon, some of the missionaries and others who have for years watched the silent, unobtrusive progress of Murray's work at Peking, deemed it necessary to publish a counter-statement of the true facts. This paper, which was published at Shanghai in the *Chinese Recorder* for June, 1891, commenced by noting how the Committee of the Shanghai Conference recommended, "*First*, a system of writing by Initials and Finals." *Secondly*, a system of spelling in the European method. While NO MENTION WAS MADE OF THE FULLY PROVEN SUCCESSFUL WORK OF MR. MURRAY.

(The system of Initials and Finals is practically spelling phonetically. It must, therefore, be separately adapted to each of the innumerable dialects of the Empire; whereas Murray's books can be read throughout all the Mandarin-speaking Provinces.

On this subject I cannot do better than quote the opinion of Dr. Stevenson of Ssu C'huan Province, a member of the Educational Committee for China. After devoting a year to the study both of the Initial and Final system, and of Murray's Numeral Type, he now gives his deliberate decision that "THE LATTER IS HEAD AND SHOULDERS ABOVE THE FORMER, AND IS GOOD FOR MANDARIN AT LEAST" (i.e. for four-fifths of the Empire).

The paper then proceeded to give a clear account of Mr. Murray's system, which is described as being "in perfect harmony with the genius of the Chinese language, which is a language of units. Every word is a unit. To divide it into syllables is unnatural. The Murray system seizes upon this distinctive feature of the language and makes it a corner-stone. Each of Murray's words represents to the pupil a perfect Chinese sound.

"It accords with the genius of the Chinese mind . . . of which . . . the one conspicuous power in activity . . . developed through a thousand years of culture, is the mechanical memory. . . . Here again, Murray's system seizes upon the mental characteristics of the people for whom it is prepared.

"NO SYMBOL IS EVER EMPLOYED FOR MORE THAN ONE PURPOSE, hence there is no confusion in the mind of the pupil, arising from the use of the same symbol, now as a mere initial, and again as an entire word.

"FINALLY THERE IS THE SUPREME TEST OF SUCCESSFUL TRIAL. The system works; boys learn it; girls learn it; it does not seem to the pupils difficult. Bright scholars master it in a fortnight; some have been known to read the Bible in a few days. Even dull ones can learn to read and write in a few months; the dullest in one year. The asylum is now in full operation. From a little girl of four, who has almost completed her primer, to men forty years of age, they may be seen reading, writing, stereotyping, printing, even writing music and reading it from their own or other's copy. Can it be that this is the system too complicated for general use throughout China!

"(Signed)   J. W. LOWRIE, *American Presb. Mission.*"

To which was appended the following postscript :—

"The above seems to us a fair and moderate view of the advantages of Murray's system for teaching the blind in

China to read and write. OF ITS SUCCESS IN PRACTICAL WORKING WE ARE ALL WITNESSES.

"(Signed) JOHN WHERRY, *American Presb. Mission.*
H. H. LOWRY, *Methodist Episcopal Mission.*
GEORGE OWEN, *London Missionary Society.*
EDWARD S. PRITCHARD, *ditto.*
WM. S. AMENT, *American Board Mission.*
S. M. RUSSELL, *Imperial College, Peking.*"

To this a final note on "the many and great advantages of Mr. Murray's system" was added by the Rev. H. Blodget, D.D.

Another very important letter was published in the *Chinese Recorder* in the spring of 1896, to refute various mis-statements regarding the Numeral Type which had been widely circulated.

The only valid ground for these attacks lay in a misunderstanding on the part of some of the advocates of the system, who at first thought that the books printed at Peking were available for the whole of China, without any alteration whatever. WHEREAS THE SYSTEM IS AT PRESENT ADAPTED ONLY TO THE USE OF THE THREE HUNDRED MILLIONS WHO SPEAK MANDARIN DIALECTS. A fair field for one man to seek to occupy! (See note on page 132.)

The letter in question replies at length to the various points raised, and says: "AT PRESENT ALL WE CAN CLAIM IS THAT MURRAY'S SYSTEM IS UNIVERSAL, WITHOUT ANY MODIFICATION, FOR ALL THE MANDARIN DIALECTS. . . . If the reader will remember that in Murray's Numeral system there are never more than two Braille elements to each word, and that no spaces are needed between the words, as each word begins with what we may call a capital letter, he will be able to realize the very great rapidity with which Murray's blind pupils can read." . . . (The finger glides swiftly over its elements, and there is no ambiguity as to where one word ends and another begins.) "Thus a degree of fluency is attainable far beyond that of any other system."

"The system is very simple, easily acquired, and requires no effort of thought in its acquirement; only a little memory."

Then with regard to teaching sighted persons, the letter goes on to say,—

"It should be remembered that the Romanized version of the Bible, and that in Murray's system, are both intended for the illiterate and those who have not time to acquire the Chinese characters. . . . Now in teaching ignorant people, why compel them to recognize Roman letters? They are not simple, and certainly not easy (to the Chinese) to write. In fact, old men and women, for whom the Romanized system is principally intended, can never hope to be able to write. With Murray's system old women can write nicely, as soon as they are able to read. It is a great advantage for converts in the country to be able to communicate by letter with the missionary.*

"(Signed)   S. M. RUSSELL, *Imperial College, Peking.*
J. DUDGEON, Esq., M.D.
Rev. W. S. AMENT, *American Board Mission.*
Rev. H. H. LOWRY, D.D., *President of the*
Rev. F. D. GAMEWELL.   [*Peking University.*
Rev. G. OWEN, *London Missionary Society.*
Rev. S. E. MEECH,   *ditto.*
Rev. J. STONEHOUSE,   *ditto.*
Rev. J. M. ALLARDYCE, M.A.,   *ditto.*"

John Dudgeon, M.D., whose long and great experience of the Chinese entitles his verdict to the greatest consideration, also wrote in the *Chinese Recorder:* "In speaking of the extent to which Murray's system can be used, what should have been said was that it was available wherever Mandarin is spoken, which is generally understood to

* The Lord's Prayer in the Romanized Chinese, Numeral Type, Shorthand, and Mandarin Chinese, will be found on pages 134, 135.

embrace four-fifths of the Empire, or say 300,000,000 of people. . . ∴. We only ask for a fair consideration of the Numeral system, the ease and rapidity with which it can be acquired, its extreme suitability to the Mandarin, and the possibility of its application to the non-Mandarin districts by the preparation of primers for each dialect or district. If the latter can be arranged, there is no reason why the system may not be adapted to these non-Mandarin speaking regions."

". . . . The Roman letters are held to be more complicated than the Murray letters. They are written with much more difficulty; the Murray system consists only of strokes and lines at right angles. It takes up almost one-third less of type-setting, one-third less of paper, one-third less of space, one-third less of freight, one-third less of storage, one-third less of duty, and so on."

". . . . When we see old women learning to read in two months, and writing to their absent missionary friends in Australia, it certainly shows a vast improvement on the old way of doing things."

Of course either Roman or Numeral type can be printed of any size. We have received samples of the latter in most minute type. THE ABOVE CALCULATION IS BASED ON TWO SAMPLES PRINTED IN TYPE OF RELATIVELY THE SAME SIZE.

Here is a truly cheering extract from the letter of a sympathetic worker in Southern China:—

"Tell Mr. Murray that there never yet was an invention (revealed by God) to ameliorate the lot of the human race, but it was cavilled at and abused, and sometimes rejected altogether, through unbelief. Tell him to take heart and take courage. If his invention is worth anything it MUST meet with opposition, that is its inevitable fate. Remind him of the fate of chloroform in surgery, of antiseptics, of printing, of the spinning-wheel, in fact I don't think there has ever been one great invention, one that would really benefit the human race, but those same stupid humans have rejected it, at any rate for a time.

"And that brings me to my second point of cheer. Such an invention is NOT man's 'invention,' but GOD'S revealing, and if HE intends it for the benefit of mankind, it cannot die, though the man who first made it known die before it be adopted or even understood; IT cannot die, and must and will take its proper place eventually in furthering the good of the human race. So bid him remember the work is not his, but God's."

Here is a valuable opinion from the Rev. R. T. Turley, of the British and Foreign Bible Society, written after a visit to the various Missions in Peking. First he describes the general work in the School for the Blind, where boys and men, girls and women, were all busy at work, reading or sorting and setting type, &c. He says: "The bright and happy look on all these was very cheering, and one easily saw the power Mr. Murray had personally gained over them by his kindly, patient disposition and exertions on their behalf."

He then visited the London Mission, and there saw a class of very ignorant, sighted Chinese women being taught to read by a blind girl. He says: "These women had been there at the most only two months, and had, I believe, only been able to give a portion of each day to the study; they could read quite nicely.... THIS VERY SIMPLE AND PRACTICAL SYSTEM OF STRAIGHT AND SQUARE MARKS RECOMMENDS ITSELF TO EVEN PREJUDICED CHINESE, WHO WILL NOT TOLERATE THE ROMANIZED.... All the old missionaries in Peking, of whom I requested an opinion concerning Mr. Murray's work, were loud and unqualified in their praise of it.... The system may not be perfect, but it is useful, easy, simple and practical, and thoroughly effective for its purpose; and many will praise the LORD for HIS faithful and hard-working servant, William Murray."

In October, 1896, the Rev. Robert Wallace, of Toronto, wrote from Chefoo to the Editor of *The Christian:* " Mrs. Wallace and I were in Peking last week, and had the privilege of seeing something of the good work in which Mr. and Mrs. Murray are engaged. We are glad to add our unqualified testimony to the real value of the work, and the need for more room for extension and development. . . . THIS IS A TRUE AND BEAUTIFUL WORK OF FAITH for a large and needy class whose lot is very hard and hopeless, and Mr. and Mrs. Murray should be cheered and encouraged by a prompt and liberal response to the appeal on behalf of the proposed improvements.

In 1896 the Rev. W. Hopkyn Rees, of the London Mission at Hsiao Chang, asked Mr. Murray to send him a blind girl to teach a class of ignorant village women. About two months later he wrote : " Quite a number of the women and girls are now quite proficient in the system and can read the Catechism and the Gospel of Mark. I enclose a note from one who has been learning for only six weeks. We have several who will be able to teach next year. We can honestly congratulate you on your successful invention. Very many thanks for the very efficient services rendered by Hannah (the blind teacher). We are all very grateful for the valuable work done."

In the following spring Mr. Rees wrote again to Mr. Murray on this subject: "IT HAS BEEN A SUCCESS ! . . . This work will be carried on every winter in future, and Miss Roberts is teaching your system at the out-stations. . . . GOD bless you and guide you to still nobler efforts for China. We are unanimous IN VOTING YOUR SYSTEM AN UNQUALIFIED SUCCESS, and an invaluable boon in teaching women and girls."

Mr. Rees followed up this letter by giving so excellent an account of his experience of the value of the system at the annual meeting of missionaries at Tientsin, that four then and there decided to adopt it.

Among the first to realize the full value of the Numeral Type was the Rev. A. H. Bridge, of Wei Chia Chuang, who sent blind pupils to be trained, and so thoroughly mastered the system himself, that so soon as Mr. Murray adapted it to the use of sighted persons, and sent sample pages to Mr. Bridge, the latter returned them, pointing out two printer's mistakes, thereby proving how carefully he had read them, and how easy is the transition from the embossed dots to the black lines.

Mr. Murray has also received most cheering letters from the Rev. H. C. Burrows, who, as he was passing through Tientsin on his way to his Mission in the Shansi Province, received a copy of the Primer, &c., from Mr. Clarke, of the Inland Mission. Without any instruction he mastered the system and taught first a seeing person, then a blind girl. The latter, in her turn, taught a seeing person, and then a blind one. This illustrates how silently the work is extending, but it fails to tell of the excellent influence on the character of those taught, which in many cases is so remarkable.

I have already referred to the thoroughly appreciative letters from the Rev. John Ross, D.D., of Manchuria, telling of the work which has already been accomplished in that vast Province by the instrumentality of blind men trained by Mr. Murray, and his conviction that many of their pupils will very soon be able to teach schools in new districts.

I will add the following from his coadjutor, the Rev. ʼJames Webster, of Manchuria, who, writing on 15th June, 1897, says: "It is the universal opinion of every missionary who has the least acquaintance with Mr. Murray's System for the Blind, that IT IS A MOST PERFECT SYSTEM FOR THE EDUCATION OF THE BLIND, and worthy of the hearty support of every Christian.

"As regards the application of the system to the Sighted,

I may say that there are diverse views as to its utility. I WENT TO PEKING PREJUDICED AGAINST IT. I LEFT PEKING WITH THE FIXED RESOLVE TO DO MY UTMOST TO INTRODUCE IT AMONGST OUR ILLITERATE CHRISTIANS IN MANCHURIA, AS BEING, IN MY OPINION, THE BEST PLAN YET OFFERED TO MAKE OUR NON-READING MEMBERS BECOME ACQUAINTED AT FIRST HAND WITH THE WORD OF GOD.

"What is needed is patience. Time alone will prove the validity of the claims made in its behalf. GIVE MURRAY AND THE REST OF US FIVE YEARS, AND I AM SATISFIED IT WILL BE A PROVED BOON TO TENS OF THOUSANDS OF ILLITERATE CHRISTIANS IN THE NORTH OF CHINA. EVERYONE WHO HAS USED MURRAY'S SYSTEM EXTOLS IT, AND NO ONE ELSE CAN SPEAK WITH ANY AUTHORITY."

Just one more extract from a letter received from the Rev. Stewart McKee, North Shansi :—

July 21st, 1897.

"For some time it has been a burden on me that our women-folk were unable to read their Bibles, and in spite of all efforts . . . not one made anything like progress. After six months of hard work (i.e. in studying Chinese ideograph), one little woman could read five chapters in St. John. That was the best. Our dialect differs so much from any in which the Testament is printed in Roman alphabet, that that system is useless for us.

"On the other hand, although this is a Mandarin-speaking district, the language is so d.fferent from book Mandarin, that it is almost another dialect, so the women cannot understand what they read, hence the difficulty.

"At last, I think I can cry, 'Eureka! I have found it!' Murray, of the National Bible Society of Scotland in Peking, has a system for the Blind, which he has also adapted for the Seeing. . . . I have set to and learned the system, and IN TWENTY-FIVE HOURS' WORK I HAD MASTERED IT SUFFICIENTLY TO READ LUKE'S GOSPEL, AND TO WRITE ANY WORD IN OUR DIALECT!

"You know there is nothing sharp in me, so THE FACT THAT I LEARNED IT SO EASILY, PROVES ITS SIMPLICITY. I am now teaching it to a class of men, who are greatly charmed with it, and Kate and the ladies are learning it in order to teach the women. In fancy I can see the day when ALL OUR WOMEN AND GIRLS WILL BE ABLE TO READ THEIR BIBLES FOR THEMSELVES, which will be a great boon indeed." . . .

This letter is especially valuable, as proving the rapidity with which the Numeral System can be acquired by a European missionary who is already thoroughly acquainted with any of the Mandarin dialects.

It would be easy to multiply similar testimonies, but I think these should suffice to convince any unbiassed mind of the value of Mr. Murray's inventions for both blind and illiterate sighted Chinese.

NOTE.—Although Mr. Murray lays stress on the point that One Version of the Scriptures printed at Peking in the Northern Mandarin dialect can be read in all the Southern Mandarin Provinces, yet in view of the fact that some of the latter have a fifth Tone, and also a much larger number of Sounds than the 408 of Peking, it seems to some of Mr. Murray's friends that it would be well that he should arrange extra numerals to represent these extra sounds, and print a Nanking Version for the Southern Mandarin Provinces.

If experience proves this to be really desirable, it can, of course, be quite easily done.

EXTRACT FROM A LETTER FROM MRS. REES.

LONDON MISSION STATION,
CHI-CHOU.

"WE have been encouraged again this year with the progress made by the women and girls who have attended the classes held annually for the instruction of our female converts. Each class stays here for a month. This year the ages range from twelve to seventy years!

"I daresay the latter figure will amaze you. What can be done for women of such an age? Can they learn anything? It used to puzzle me, but it is wonderful how quickly they learn. Love and patience make them courageous and confident. . . . It is such a joy to see how God's Words take root in their hearts, and the fruits of the Spirit then begin to grow steadily. They return home with truer ideas of right and wrong. Unkind and hasty words are few, and quickly repented of.

"This year I have had my bright women taught the 'Murray' system of reading. Mr. Murray was kind enough to send me one of his blind teachers. It is marvellous how much the women can learn in such a short time. Some have learned in six weeks to read the Catechism, St. Mark, and St. John's Gospels. They seemed much interested in it, and I believe this new system will, under God's blessing, be productive of much good. TEN OF THE WOMEN, AND ALL THE SCHOOLGIRLS HAVE ENTIRELY MASTERED IT IN LESS THAN SIX WEEKS, and can now read MOST OF THE BOOKS THAT ARE PRINTED IN THE 'MURRAY'

TYPE. Last night one of them wrote me a letter, and with the help of the book, I was able to make out every word.

"THIS IS BY FAR THE EASIEST WAY OF TEACHING THE WOMEN OF CHINA TO READ, and if I had the funds I would invite another batch of women here to learn before the busy season begins. The women taught this year will be able next year to teach others.

"My heart yearns to be able to keep up this plan of work for a few months longer, but alas! I have no more funds. FIVE OF THE WOMEN BROUGHT THEIR OWN FOOD AND FIREWOOD, AND ONE WOMAN BROUGHT FOOD FOR HERSELF AND ANOTHER. This is a step in the right direction, and MANY WISH THEY COULD DO SO, BUT THEY ARE TOO POOR, AND CANNOT KEEP TWO HOMES GOING."

The Rev. A. H. Bridge, who is working alone in the large district of Wei-Chên, sends a most interesting account of the work already done by his first blind convert, Ssŭ Yungkuei, an able and exemplary man, who has for some time been working as an Evangelist in sole charge of a district, sixteen miles to the south of Wei-Chên. With the help of a nephew, trained by himself, he has gathered quite a large congregation of earnest converts, whom he has convinced of the truth " by simple preaching and arguments " from the Scriptures, placed in his hands by the wonderful " invention of Mr. Murray. He does real good solid work, " and is a man in whom I have every confidence. He is now " about forty years of age, and he became blind when he was " about twenty. He was converted about eight years ago."

LATEST NEWS FROM MANCHURIA.

WHEN the missionaries of Manchuria met in Conference at the close of 1897, the merits of the Numeral Type were among the subjects for discussion, and the following resolutions were unanimously adopted :—

"THE COMMITTEE ARE UNANIMOUSLY OF OPINION THAT MR. MURRAY'S SYSTEM HAS PROVED ITSELF TO BE WELL ADAPTED FOR TEACHING THE BLIND.

"From reports from various sources the Committee have learned that Mr. Murray's System, as applied to the teaching of illiterate Sighted, has produced very gratifying results.

"The Committee are of opinion that a School for the Blind, on a small scale, might with advantage be established in Moukden.

"THE COMMITTEE RECOMMEND THAT ANY MISSIONARY DESIRING TO MAKE A TRIAL OF THE SYSTEM, AS ADAPTED TO THE ILLITERATE SIGHTED, SHOULD BE ENCOURAGED TO DO SO."

AN EXPLANATION

OF

Mr. MURRAY'S SYSTEM

FOR

TEACHING ILLITERATE SIGHTED CHINESE

BY

PROFESSOR S. M. RUSSELL, M.A.
Imperial College Peking.

THE LORD'S PRAYER IN MANDARIN CHINESE.

1. IN ROMAN ALPHABET, according to Sir Thomas Wade's standard spelling. This requires to be altered to suit each dialect in every Province.

Wo³ mên¹ tsai⁴ t' iên¹ shang⁴ ti¹ fu⁴,
yüan⁴ jên² tu¹ tsun¹ Ni³ ti¹ ming⁴ wei⁴ sheng⁴,
yüan⁴ Ni³ ti¹ kuo² chiang⁴ lin²,
yuan⁴ Ni³ ti¹ chih³ yi⁴ hsing² tsai⁴ ti⁴ shang⁴,
ju² t' ung² hsing² tsai⁴ t' ien¹ shang⁴.
Wo³ men¹ jih⁴ yung⁴ ti¹ yin³ shih²,
chin¹ jih⁴ t' su⁴ yü³ wo³ mên¹,
miên³ wo³ mên¹ ti¹ chai⁴,
ju² t' ung² wo³ mên¹ mien³ jên² ti¹ chai⁴.
Pu⁴ chao⁴ wo³ mên¹ yü⁴ chiên⁴ shih⁴ t' an⁴,
chiu⁴ wo³ mên¹ t' o¹ li² hsiung¹ ê⁴,
yin¹ wei¹ kuo² tu⁴ c' hūan¹ ping³ jung² yūeh⁴ c' hūan¹ shih⁴ ni³ ti¹
shih⁴ shih⁴ wu² c' hiung² a¹ mên¹.

2. IN THE NUMERAL TYPE, wh'ch can be read with equal facility in all Provinces of Mandarin China—which comprises eight-ninths of the whole of China—without any alteration, except, in certain Provinces, the addition of a very simple symbol to denote a fifth tone. (See note on page 132.)

THE LORD'S PRAYER IN MANDARIN CHINESE.

3. In Shorthand for Numeral Type.

4. The Lord's Prayer in Mandarin Chinese as pronounced at Peking.

我們在天上的父願
人都尊你的名為聖
願你的國降臨願你
的旨意行在地上如
同行在天上我們日
用的飲食求你今日
賜給我們免我們的
債如同我們免人的
債不叫我們遇見試
探救我們脫離兇惡
因為國度權柄榮耀
全是你的世世無窮

EXPLANATION OF MR. MURRAY'S SYSTEM FOR TEACHING SIGHTED CHINESE TO READ AND WRITE.

For many years the Rev. W. H. Murray, agent of the National Bible Society of Scotland, has worked among the Blind in China. No one who has visited his school in Peking can have failed to have been struck with the rapidity and correctness with which his pupils read and write.

Owing to his great success in teaching the blind, Mr. Murray conceived the idea that the same system might be readily acquired by illiterate men and women, who, although endowed with sight, had not the time or ability to learn the Chinese hieroglyphics.

As the system for the Seeing and the Blind are exactly the same in principle, I shall explain the former only.

There are 408 sounds in the Chinese Mandarin dialect. These sounds are given in Table A, in rows of ten characters. The first and last rows contain only nine characters.

Above each character is written its number in the series, from No. 1 to 408.

Below each character is written its pronunciation in the Pekingese dialect; but of course a person in, say Shantung, would give the Shantung pronunciation.

Underneath the pronunciation of each character is its symbol in Mr. Murray's notation, representing numerals.

TABLE A. No. 1.

司 Ssu	10 戰 -Chan ˋ	1 阿 ˉ	2 愛 Ai ˋ	3 安 An ˉ	4 昂 Ang ˊ	5 傲 Ao ˋ	6 扎 Cha ˉ	7 扱 C'ha ˉ	8 寨 Chai ˋ	9 差 Ch'ai ˉ
弟 Ti	20 正 -Chêng ˋ	11 禪 Ch'an ˊ	12 杖 Chang ˋ	13 常 Ch'ang ˊ	14 昭 Chao ˉ	15 朝 Ch'ao ˊ	16 這 Chê ˋ	17 車 Ch'ê ˉ	18 眞 Chên ˉ	19 沉 Ch'ên ˊ
尼 Ni	30 姐 -Chieh ˇ	21 成 Ch'êng ˊ	22 際 Chi ˋ	23 其 Ch'i ˊ	24 家 Chia ˉ	25 恰 Ch'ia ˋ	26 將 Chiang ˉ	27 嬙 Ch'iang ˊ	28 交 Chiao ˉ	29 瞧 Ch'iao ˊ
迷 Mi	40 絕 -Chüeh ˊ	31 妾 Ch'ieh ˋ	32 見 Chien ˋ	33 淺 Ch'ien ˇ	34 知 Chih ˉ	35 吃 Ch'ih ˉ	36 金 Chin ˉ	37 親 Ch'in ˉ	38 井 Ching ˇ	39 淸 Ch'ing ˉ
入 Ju		41 礁 Ch'üeh ˋ	42 酒 Chiu ˇ	43 囚 Ch'iu ˊ	44 蒼 Chiung ˉ	45 窮 Ch'iung ˊ	46 椊 Cho ˉ	47 綽 Ch'o ˋ	48 粥 Chou ˉ	49 稠 Ch'ou ˊ

TABLE A. No. 2.

離 Li	50 居 -Cüi	51 麴 Ch'ü	52 圈 Chüan	53 囷 Ch'üan	54 埈 Chün	55 薮 Ch'ün	56 嚼 Chüeh	57 柱 Chu	58 出 Ch'u	59 抓 Chua.
閃 Shan	60 㕦 -Ch'ua	61 拽 Chuai	62 躋 Ch'uai	63 磚 Chuan	64 川 Ch'uan	65 庄 Chuang	66 窗 Ch'uang	67 墜 Chui	68 垂 Ch'ui	69 準 Chun.
苦 K'u	70 䑛 -Ch'un	71 衆 Chung	72 冲 Ch'ung	73 擲 Ch'uo	74 惡 O,	75 恩 Ên	76 哼 Êng	77 兒 Êrh	78 法 Fa	79 犯 Fan.
非 Fei	80 方 -Fang	81 費 Fei	82 粉 Fên	83 風 Fêng	84 佛 Fo,	85 否 Fou	86 復 Fu	87 哈 Ha	88 咳 Hai	89 汗 Han.
跛 Po	90 悲 -Hang	91 好 Hao	92 黑 Hei	93 很 Hen	94 恆 Hêng,	95 河 Ho	96 後 Hou	97 湖 Hu	98 化 Hua	99 瑷 Huai.

TABLE A. No. 3.

Group										
打算 T'a Suan	100 換 'Huan	101 黃 'Huang	102 灰 'Hui	103 渾 'Hun	104 紅 'Hung	105 火 'Huo	106 夕 Hsi	107 下 Hsia	108 相 Hsiang	109 小 Hsiao
他當 T'a Tang	110 謝 -Hsieh	111 先 Hsien	112 心 Hsin	113 性 Hsing	114 學 Hsüeh	115 修 Hsiu	116 兄 Hsiung	117 虛 Hsü	118 旋 Hsüan	119 雪 Hsüeh
他能 T'a Neng	120 訓 -Hsün	121 孝 Hsiao	122 衣 I	123 染 Jan	124 嚷 Jang,	125 饒 Jao	126 惹 Jê	127 人 Jên		129 日 Jih
他們 T'a Mên	130 弱 -Jo	131 肉 Jou	132 入 Ju	133 輭 Juan	134 瑞 Jui,	135 潤 Jun	136 容 Jung	137 喀 Ka	138 該 Kai	139 凱 K'ai
天然 T'ien Jan	140 乾 -Kan	141 扶 K'an	142 岡 Kang	143 康 K'ang	144 給 Kei,	145 根 Kên	146 肯 K'ên	147 更 Keng	148 坑 K'eng	149 哥 Ke

140

TABLE A. No. 4.

都 來 Tu Lai	150 客 -K'ê	151 溝 Kou	152 口 K'ou	153 古 Ku	154 苦 K'u	155 瓜 Kua	156 跨 K'ua	157 怪 Kuai	158 快 K'uai	159 管 Kuan.
他 使 T'a Shih	160 欸 -K'uan	161 光 Kuang	162 筐 K'uang	163 貴 Kuei	164 魁 K'uei,	165 棍 Kun	166 坤 K'un	167 工 Kung	168 恐 K'ung	169 過 Kuo.
大 工 Ta Kung	170 闊 -K'uo	171 臘 La	172 來 Lai	173 爛 Lan	174 稂 Lang,	175 老 Lao	176 樂 Le	177 累 Lei	178 徒 Leng	179 歷 Li.
大 扁 Ta Fu	180 倆 -Lia	181 糧 Liang	182 料 Liao	183 列 Lieh	184 連 Lien,	185 林 Lin	186 令 Ling	187 略 Lüo	188 留 Liu	189 落 Lo.
搭 棚 Ta P'eng	190 樓 -Lou	191 驢 Lü	192 戀 Lüan	193 掄 Lün	194 路 Lü,	195 亂 Luan	196 論 Lun	197 龍 Lung	198 馬 Ma	199 買 Mai.

TABLE A. No. 5.

	200	201	202	203	204,	205	206	207	208	209.
你 Ni 須 Hsū	慢 Man	忙 Mang	毛 Mao	美 Mei	門 Men,	夢 Meng	迷 Mi	廟 Miao	滅 Mieh	免 Mien.
	210	211	212	213	214,	215	216	217	218	219.
你 Ni 當 Tang	民 -Min	明 Ming	謬 Mui	磨 Mo	謀 Mou,	木 Mu	拿 Na	奶 Nai	南 Nan	囊 Nang.
	220	221	222	223	224,	225	226	227	228	229.
你 Ni 難 Nan	腦 -Nao	內 Nei	能 Neng	尼 Ni	娘 Niang,	鳥 Niao	乜 Nieh	年 Nien	您 Nin	寧 Ning.
	230	231	232	233	234,	235	236	237	238	239.
你 Ni 免 Mien	虐 -Nio	牛 Niu	挪 No	耨 Nou	女 Nü,	奴 Nu	暖 Nuan	嫩 Nun	濃 Nung	訛 O.
	240	241	242	243	244,	245	246	247	248	249.
你 Ni 惹 Jo	偶 -Ou	罷 Pa	怕 P'a	拜 Pai	派 P'ai,	辦 Pan	盼 P'an	挪 Pang	旁 P'ang	包 Pao.

141

TABLE A. No. 6.

那 Na 里 Li	250 跑 -P'ao	251 碑 Pei	252 培 P'ei	253 本 Pen	254 盆 P'en,	255 崩 Peng	256 朋 P'eng	257 必 Pi	258 擘 P'i	259 表 Piao.
你 Ni 使 Shih	260 票 -P'iao	261 別 Pieh	262 撇 P'ieh	263 匾 Pien	264 片 P'ien,	265 賓 Pin	266 品 P'in	267 兵 Ping	268 平 P'ing	269 魄 Po.
你 Ni 敢 Kan	270 破 -P'o	271 布 Pu	272 舖 P'u	273 撒 Sa	274 賽 Sai,	275 散 San	276 桑 Sang	277 掃 Sao	278 色 Sê	279 森 Sên.
能 Neng 罰 Fa	280 僧 Sêng	281 索 So	282 搜 Sou	283 素 Su	284 算 Suan,	285 歲 Sui	286 孫 Sun	287 送 Sung	288 殺 Sha	289 曬 Shai.
你 Ni 背 Pei	290 善 -Shan	291 上 Shang	292 燒 Shao	293 蛇 Shê	294 伸 Shên	295 生 Shêng	296 是 Shih	297 手 Shou	298 書 Shu	299 刷 Shua.

TABLE A. No. 7.

	300 撳 -Shuai	301 拴 Shuan	302 雙 Shuang	303 誰 Shui	304, 順 Shun,	305 說 Shuo	306 似 Ssu	307 大 Ta	308 他 T'a	309. 代 Tai.
馬 鬆 Ma Sung										
	310 大 -Tai	311 但 Tan	312 談 T'an	313 當 Tang	314, 堂 T'ang,	315 道 Tao	316 討 T'ao	317 德 Tê	318 登 Têng	319. 騰 T'êng.
迷 謎 Mi T'an										
	320 遞 -Ti	321 提 T'i	322 吊 Tiao	323 挑 T'iao	324, 疊 Tieh,	325 帖 T'ieh	326 典 Tien	327 添 T'ien	328 定 Ting	329. 聽 T'ing.
汝 難 Mei Nan										
	330 丟 -Tiu	331 多 To	332 馱 T'o	333 豆 Tou	334, 頭 T'ou,	335 都 Tu	336 圖 T'u	337 短 Tuan	338 團 T'uan	339. 對 Tui.
買 賣 Mai Mai										
	340 推 T'ui	341 敦 Tun	342 屯 T'un	343 東 Tung	344, 通 T'ung,	345 雜 Tsa	346 搽 Ts'a	347 在 Tsai	348 財 Ts'ai	349. 簪 Tsan.
汝 嚷 Mei Jang										

TABLE A. No. 8.

	350 嘶 ‑Tsan	351 賊 Tsang	352 倉 T'sang	353 造 Tsao	354 草 T'sao,	355 宅 Tsê	356 災 T'sê	357 賊 Tsei	358 增 Tsêng,	359 層 T'sêng,
沒理 Mei Li										
	360 作 ‑Tso	361 錯 T'so	362 走 Tsou	363 諛 T'sou	364 足 Tsu,	365 醋 T'su,	366 鑽 Tsuan	367 躦 T'suan	368 嘴 Tsui	369 崔 T'sui,
沒食 Mei Shih										
	370 伶 ‑Tsun	371 村 T'sun	372 總 Tsung	373 從 T'sung	374 子 Tsŭ	375 蒸 T'sŭ	376 娃 Wa	377 外 Wai	378 玩 Wan	379 柾 Wang.
矇告 Mengkao										
	380 位 ‑Wei	381 問 Wên	382 翁 Wêng	383 我 Wo	384 無 Wu,	385 牙 Ya	386 埃 Yai	387 羊 Yang	388 遙 Yao	389 野 Yeh.
民分 Min Fen										
	390 言 ‑Yen	391 義 Yi	392 音 Yin	393 應 Ying	394 約 Yüeh,	395 餘 Yü	396 原 Yüan	397 月 yüeh	398 云 Yün	399 有 Ye.
朋白 Mung Pai										
	400 用 ‑Yung	401 告 Kao	402 靠 K'ao	403 得 Tei	404 咱 Tsên	405 付 T'sên	406 特 Tê	407 塞 Sai	408 抛 P'ou	
如斯 Ju Ssu										

, The first thing for the pupil to do is to learn by heart these 408 sounds, and the number corresponding to each tenth sound. For instance, he must remember that 390 is Yen, that 160 is K'uan, and so on. Mr. Murray makes this comparatively easy by a system of Mnemonics, which I shall now explain.

SYSTEM OF MNEMONICS FOR LEARNING THE 408 SOUNDS.

In Table A, at the beginning of each line, and forming a separate column, are placed the characters Ssu, Ti, Ni, Mi, &c.* These are the Mnemonic sounds, and stand for numbers.

In Table B, I give the Mnemonic sounds in ten squares.

The sounds in the first square, *Tan, Ti*, &c., all represent One ; *Ni, Na, Nan,* in the second square, all stand for two, and so on. Those in the tenth square, *Hsü, Ssû, Suan,* all stand for the 0, as in 200, 300, &c.

The pupil first learns Table B thoroughly, so that if the teacher says 5, the pupil at once repeats *Lai, Li,* &c. ; or if the teacher says 8, the pupil answers, *Fen, Fa,* &c. ; or if the teacher says *Ling,* the pupil answers, *Hsü, Ssû, Suan ;* and *vice versâ* if the teacher says *Pai,* the pupil answers 9.

Having learned Table B thoroughly, the pupil learns Table A.

METHOD OF LEARNING TABLE A.

The pupil begins by learning the Mnemonic sound, coupled with the first sound in each row of ten, as Ssu A (1), Ti Chan (10), Ni Cheng (20), Mi Chieh (30), Ju Chüeh (40), Ta suan Huan (100), Ju Ssu-yung (400). Nearly all of these have a meaning which helps to fix it in the memory.

* Of course these Chinese characters are only for the use of the teacher, from whose lips the illiterate pupil learns the sound represented.

SYSTEM OF MNEMONICS FOR LEARNING THE 408 SOUNDS.

A glance at Table A shows at the beginning of each line the characters *Ssu*, *Ti*, *Ni*, *Mi*, &c. These are the Mnemonic sounds, and stand for numbers. In Table B I give the Mnemonic sounds in ten squares:—

TABLE B.

一 但弟當打他都談大天 四 入然如喏熱 七 敢告苦工	二 你尼那難能 五 來離裡呂 八 分罰非痛 零 許司斯算	三 迷門馬沒明蒙民 六 韭使閃 九 白背跋棚

The sounds in the 1st square, *Tan*, *Ti*, &c., all represent One. *Ni*, *Na*, *Nan*, in the 2nd square, all stand for Two, and so on. Those in the 10th square, *Hsü*, *Ssu*, *Suan*, all stand for the o, as in 200.

This must be learned thoroughly, so that if the teacher says, for instance, *T'a Shih*, the pupil at once says, *K'uan* (160), or *vice versâ*.

The use of Mnemonics in Table B is now evident; for instance, if the pupil says *T'a Men Jo*, he knows at once that *Jo* is the 130th sound; for *T'a* stands for 1, and *Men* for 3, and likewise for all the others.

Having now learned the first sound in each row, according to the above method, the pupil learns each row of ten separately, as *A, Ai, An*, &c., and Chan, Ch'an, Chang, &c.

The teacher should now question the pupil as to his knowledge of Table A. For instance, if he asks what is the 64th sound, the pupil should at once recollect that 6 is the Mnemonic *Shan*, and so *Ch'ua* is 60, and counting 4 further on, get *Ch'uan* for 64. At the beginning the pupil must so count, but with a little practice, the mental process is performed with almost automatic rapidity, and the eye learns to recognize the symbol, as quickly as a Chinese scholar recognizes a character.*

NOTATION.

According to Mr. Murray's system, instead of writing the sound, the pupil writes only the number of the sound as given in Table A.

For the Blind, Mr. Murray uses Braille's elements (i.e. embossed dots). For the Seeing, the dots in Braille's elements are joined by lines. The Notation for the Seeing exactly corresponds with that for the Blind.

Thus the Blind can set up the type, and prepare books for those endowed with Sight.

Table C shows the elements used for the Blind, and Table D those used for the Seeing.

* Or a British schoolboy seeing eight or ten letters of the alphabet, all with totally different sounds, does not say them, but recognizes at a glance the word which they represent, e.g. THOROUGHLY, YACHT, COMPARATIVELY, &c.

TABLE C.
For the Blind.

Embossed in white dots.

TABLE D.

LARGE OR DOUBLE LETTERS.			SMALL OR SINGLE LETTERS.
310 to 408	210 to 309	110 to 209	
⸱⸴ ⌐	⸱⸱ ⌐	⸲ ⌐	⸱ (1)
⸲⸴ ⌐	∟ ⌐	⌊ ⌐	∣ (2)
⁻⸴ ⌐	⸗ ⌐	⁻⸴ ⌐	⁻ (3)
⌐⸴ ⌐	⌐⸴ ⌐	⌐⸴ ⌐	⌐ (4)
⸜⸴ ⌐	⸜⸍ ⌐	⸜⸴ ⌐	⸜ (5)
⌈⸴ ⌐	⌈⸲ ⌐	⌈⸴ ⌐	⌈ (6)
▢⸴ ⌐	▢ ⌐	▢⸴ ⌐	▢ (7)
⌊⸴ ⌐	⌊⸲ ⌐	⌊⸴ ⌐	⌊ (8)
⸝⸴⸱ ⌐	⸝⸝ ⌐	⸝⸴ ⌐	⸝ (9)
⌐⸴ ⌐	⌐⸲ ⌐	⌐⸴ ⌐	⌐ (0)
⸝			

For details see Table A.

How the Tones are Indicated.

The sounds in Table A, from one to nine inclusive, are indicated by one single letter, so that there is one space left vacant. High or low to the left indicate 1st or 2nd tone, and high or low to the right, the 3rd or 4th tone. For instance, sound No. 1 a in the four tones is expressed as follows :—

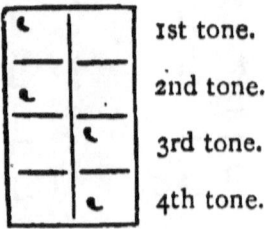

1st tone.
2nd tone.
3rd tone.
4th tone.

All sounds from the 10th to the 109th are expressed by two single letters. Both letters high, indicate the 1st tone; both low, the 2nd tone. First letter low, second high, the 3rd tone, and the reverse the 4th tone.

Thus the nineteenth sound, *Ch'en*, is expressed in the four tones as follows :—

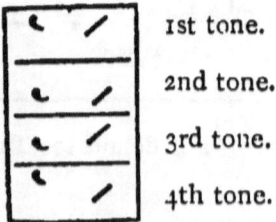

1st tone.
2nd tone.
3rd tone.
4th tone.

All sounds from 1st to 109th, that is, those expressed by small or single letters, are read from *left* to *right*.

All sounds from 110th to the end consist, as we have seen, of a large or double letter, and a small or single.

The small letter on the left, high or low, indicates 1st or 2nd tone. The small letter on the right, high or low, indicates the 3rd or 4th tone. Thus for the 1st or 2nd tone we read from right to left, and for the 3rd or 4th tone, from left to right. In fact we always read from the double letter. As an example I give the 287th sound Sung in the 4 tones :—

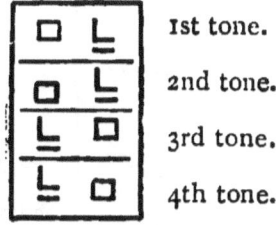

1st tone.
2nd tone.
3rd tone.
4th tone.

I have gone into the above at full length, but one learns in a few minutes the notation, and the method of indicating the tones. Since this was written Mr. Murray has added a very simple symbol to denote the 5th tone, which occurs in certain Provinces.

An easy reading lesson is next given, with the number in our notation and the corresponding sound and tone.

Thus ▢ ⌊ is 127, 2nd tone, as small letter is low on the left, and looking up Table A we see that the 127th sound is "$jên^2$". ⏤ ⏋ is 34, 1st tone, as small letter is high on the left. After some practice in reading, the pupil recognizes a symbol directly without thinking of the number it represents. Indeed, he recognizes the symbol as a Chinaman recognizes a character.

Note.—In certain Provinces a 5th tone occurs. Mr. Murray has devised a special symbol to express this.

READING LESSON.

chiao	教	28		jên	人	127	
chih	之	34		chih	之	34	
tao	道	315		ch'u	初	53	
kuei	貴	163		hsing	性	113	
yi	以	391		pên	本	253	
chuan	專	63		shan	善	290	
hsi	昔	106		hsing	性	113	
mêng	孟	205		hsiang	相	108	
mu	母	215		chin	近	36	
tsê	擇	355		hsi	習	106	
lin	鄰	185		hsiang	相	108	
ch'u	處	58		yüan	遠	296	
tsŭ	子	374		kou	苟	151	
pu	不	274		pu	不	271	
hsüeh	學	114		chiao	教	28	
tuan	斷	337		hsing	性	113	
chi	機	22		nai	乃	217	
chu	杼	57		ch'ien	遷	33	

ADVANTAGES OF MR. MURRAY'S SYSTEM.

It is quite as easily learnt as the Romanized—indeed more easily. Once acquired it can be read much more fluently and correctly. As each word consists of only two letters (or parts), they catch the eye at once, whereas in the Romanized the eye has to glance over several letters forming one word.

In the Romanized system the sound is indicated by a system of initials and finals, so that it is often very difficult to represent the exact sound. In Mr. Murray's system the sound is learned from Table A by means of the Chinese Character,* and is therefore exact.

As it stands, Mr. Murray's system is a universal one for all Mandarin dialects, and by certain modifications it might be adapted to all other dialects. (See note on page 132.)

The pupil learns the 408 sounds direct from the character in Table A. A man of Peking would give his pronunciation, a person from Shantung would give his, one from Nanking his, and so on for the other Mandarin-speaking districts.

Now in the Romanized system a new orthography would be necessary for almost every district. A version in Pekingese would be unintelligible in Shantung, and *vice versâ*. For example, in the list of sounds in Table A, number 170 is pronounced K'uo in Peking; fifty miles to the south it is pronounced K'ê. Now in the Romanized system such a change of dialect involves great confusion, but in Mr. Murray's system all difficulty disappears. The man of Peking sees the symbol, and reads it K'uo, whilst the man from the country reads it as K'ê, and to each it conveys precisely the same meaning.

* As previously stated, these Chinese characters, or ideographs, are only for the use of the teacher. It is not necessary for the pupil to know a single character. He has only to master the different sounds.

As each word consists of two letters only, inclusive of tone, books in this system can be printed very cheaply, whereas in the Romanized many words consist of five or six letters, and in addition, aspirates and tones have to be indicated, so that books in the Romanized system must necessarily be bulky and expensive.

The blind can set up the type and print for the seeing, and thus suitable employment may be found for the blind boys and girls in the various Missions.

Another advantage is that Mr. Murray's system is very easily written. A lady who has taught the Romanized tells me that in future she will never teach her women to write, as it is so difficult for them to learn. Whereas the very first class of country women who learned Mr. Murray's system for a period of three months (and who did not begin to learn to write till they had been learning the system for about seven weeks), found that they were able to write letters to their teachers, the writing being good, as well as correct.

The Rev. W. H. Murray's Mission
TO THE
Blind and Illiterate in China.

OFFICE-BEARERS AND COMMITTEE.

Chairman.
Rev. J. ELDER CUMMING, D.D.

Vice-Chairman.
T. BROWN HENDERSON, Esq., M.D.

Committee.

J. WALLACE ANDERSON, Esq., M.D.
THOS. BARR, Esq., M.D.
Rev. JAS. BLACK, D.D.
Rev. WILLIAM BOYD, LL.D.
Rev. G. L. CARSTAIRS.
Rev. JOSEPH CORBETT, D.D.
Major HOTCHKIS.
Miss C. F. GORDON-CUMMING, Crieff, Scotland.

Rev. J. MARSHALL LANG, D.D.
DAVID LOCKHART, Esq.
Rev. JAS. RENNIE.
Rev. JOHN RIDDELL, B.A.
Rev. JOHN SLOAN.
Rev. W. ROSS TAYLOR, D.D.
ANDERSON ROBERTSON, Esq., M.A. Oxon.
Mrs. DUNCAN McLAREN, St. Oswalds, Edinburgh.

Hon. Secretary.
JOHN GRANT, Esq., B.L., *Writer*,
102, BATH STREET, GLASGOW.

Treasurer.
JAMES DRUMMOND, Esq., *Chartered Accountant*,
58, BATH STREET, GLASGOW.

PEKING LOCAL COMMITTEE.

Hon. Treasurer.
Professor S. M. RUSSELL, *Imperial College, Peking.*

Rev. H. H. LOWRY, D.D., *President of the Peking University.*
Rev. J. W. LOWRIE, *American Presbyterian Mission.*
Rev. J. M. ALLARDYCE, M.A., *London Missionary Society.*
Rev. GEORGE OWEN, *London Missionary Society.*

Rev. W. S. AMENT, *American Board of Missions.*
JOHN DUDGEON, Esq., M.D., *Peking.*
The Rev. WILLIAM H. MURRAY, *School for the Blind.*
The Rev. W. HOSKYNS REES, *London Missionary Society.*
(*Corresponding members*).

Mission to the Chinese Blind.

REGULATIONS FOR THE MANAGEMENT OF THE BUSINESS OF THE SOCIETY.

Drawn up by the Committee in 1894.

I. The object of the Mission shall be to originate and maintain Institutions for employing the Chinese blind, teaching them to read and print or distribute the Scriptures and other Christian literature in the Chinese tongue; and generally to promote and develop the systems invented or employed by the Rev. W. H. Murray, whether for the benefit of blind or sighted persons in China.

II. The charge of the Mission, including the funds and the direction of all serious expenditure, shall continue to be in the hands of the present Committee, who shall have power to fill up vacancies as they occur in their number, from the subscribers to the funds. The Committee shall consist in future of not less than ten persons; and shall meet in Glasgow at least twice in the year—five to be a quorum.

III. The Committee shall appoint an Acting Committee, whose duty it shall be to transact all ordinary business, and which shall consist of at least four persons, with the Chairman, Treasurer, and Secretary, *ex officiis*—four to be a quorum.

IV. The procedure of the Acting Committee shall be subject to the review of the General Committee; and a special meeting of the General Committee shall be summoned at any time on the written request of any two members of the Acting Committee.

V. The Chairman, at all meetings, shall have a deliberative and a casting vote.

VI. The General Committee shall appoint a Local Committee in China, to advise and co-operate with Mr. Murray in developing the various branches of his work; and this Local Committee shall have power to carry out such details and sanction such minor expenditure as may be deemed suitable. Minutes of their transactions shall be submitted quarterly to the Acting Committee in Glasgow.

VII. The Committee shall endeavour to secure an adequate Endowment Fund, and Annual Subscriptions for the maintenance and development of the work.

VIII. The accounts shall be audited annually by two Auditors appointed by the Committee.

IX. A Public Meeting of the Friends of the Mission shall be held from time to time, as may be deemed advisable, and a report of the Society's proceedings submitted to it.

FINANCE.

"Seeds that mildew in the garner,
Scattered, fill with gold the plain."

THE sole property of this Mission consists of the recently acquired premises, and a small Endowment Fund, which at the close of 1897 amounts to a little over £4000, yielding about £130 interest, towards securing Mr. Murray's salary.

FOR ALL OTHER PURPOSES.—Maintenance of Blind students, upkeep of buildings, development of Mr. Murray's inventions for the illiterate Sighted, salary of a Matron for the Blind Girls' School, and of a much-needed assistant for Mr. Murray—in short, for extension of work in any direction, this Mission is wholly dependent on very fluctuating donations, and a VERY FEW ANNUAL SUBSCRIPTIONS.

It is greatly to be desired that the latter should largely increase in number, and that many Churches and Schools should undertake to collect an annual sum for the support of one Blind Student or Teacher. About £10 annually suffices for this purpose.

Who will give £300 to secure his own permanent representative in this Mission? I doubt whether it would be possible to find any investment which, from a Missionary point of view, is more certain to prove remunerative.

It is much to be desired that the great Societies which have established Missions IN THE MANDARIN-SPEAKING PROVINCES OF CHINA should now authorize and recommend their Agents at many stations to incur the expenses necessary for sending some of their own illiterate converts, both blind and sighted, to Peking, to be taught and trained as evangelists, teachers, organists, and printers, and then sent back to their own villages to start schools there among their own poor neighbours.

It is also essential that a grant should be made to support these for the first few years, as at first the scholars will be almost exclusively very poor persons, each of whom, however, will almost certainly become a very practical Home Missionary, and thus the "little leaven" will spread till by degrees it "leavens the whole lump."

In no other country have so many converts attributed the conviction which has induced them to face all the persecution that almost invariably follows the renunciation of idolatry, solely to their solitary study of some copy of the Scriptures which has casually fallen into their hands. If this has been the case where so small a proportion of the people are able to read, how certain will be the increase of converts when this extraordinarily simple method of printing and of learning to read, places the Holy Book within easy reach of all?

Friends who desire to transmit their gifts direct to the Mission-field, can do so by payment to the Hong Kong and Shanghai Banking Co. in London, for transmission to the Local Treasurer's account with their branch in Peking.

Form of Bequest.

Those who wish to remember the Mission in their last Will and Testament, are requested to use the following FORM OF BEQUEST.

I GIVE and bequeath to Mr. Murray's Mission to the Chinese Blind, and to promote and develop the systems invented by him, whether for the benefit of Blind or Sighted persons in China, the sum of (*to be inserted in words*), to be paid, free of all Government Duties, to the Treasurer or Treasurers for the time being of said Mission, whose receipt of discharge for the same shall be sufficient.

INDEX.

ABACUS, 64
Accidental loss of arm, 11
Allardyce, Mrs., 95-98
Alphabet, foreign, repugnant, 101, 126
Ancestral Worship, 60
Angular forms acceptable to Chinese, 7, 101
Apt pupils, 72, 73, 96
Arithmetic, mental, 63

BELL'S visible speech, 20
Birth, 11
Blindness, why so common, 17
Blind, the, manner of life, 18
—— left to starve, 27
—— saved from suffocation, 39
—— from poison, 55
—— from drowning, 56
—— first pupils, 26, 29
—— Peter, 40-43
—— School, 64, 70, 71
Braille's System, 22
British and Foreign Bible Society, 33, 34

CAREY, the Baptist cobbler, 13
Cargill and Cross land in Fiji, 13
Catalogue, 160
Ch'ang of Manchuria, 75-88
—— his dream, 79
—— his memory, 88
Chicago, cremation of my books, 92
China, starts for, 14

Chinese ideograph, 14
Christie, Doctor, 76
Classic of Jesus, 16, 19
Coffin, a post of honour, 15
College of Glasgow, attends classes at, 14
Colporteur, is engaged as a, 12
Colporteur's experiences, 15, 16, 67. 68
Committee formed in 1887, 51
—— members of, in 1897, 133
—— constitution of, 155
Consumption, deaths from, 71, 72

DELAYS, 91
Dudgeon, Doctor, 28, 126
—— Mina, 22

EMPEROR'S early levees, 29
Explanation, 6, 7
Extemporized Map of China, 8

FINANCE, 156, 157
First formal recognition, 51
Floods in China, 67
Fluency in reading, 66, 126
Foreign ships, work among, 12
Forget-me-nots, 85

GEOGRAPHY for the blind, 63

HOME, 11, 110
Hsii, organist, 73-75
Hun Yuen sect, 75, 76
Hymn with music, 87, 97

I.

INDEX

INDIAN ink, note, 101
Infirmary required, 66

JAPAN, war with, 107
Jubilee, my own, 50
—— Fund, how apportioned, 52

LARGE number of sounds in Southern Mandarin, 132
Lee, blind pupil, 26
Livingstone, the Glasgow cotton-piecer, 14
Literary honour, practical, 27
Little Scripture readers, 65
London Medical Mission at Peking, 28

MANCHURIA, 75
—— first blind school in, 87
Mandarin dialects, note, 9, 99
—— number of sounds in, 20
Map on tin sheets, 62
Marriage, 52
Marsham, bookseller's apprentice, 13
Massage not practised, 103
Memory, retentive, 41, 64, 87, 88
Mnemonics, 24, 41, 63
Moon's alphabet for the blind, 20
Morrison begins work in China, 13
Murray, birth, 11
—— post-office work, 11
—— colporteur, 12
—— college, 14
—— sails for China, 14
—— his vision, 22
—— first pupils, 26, 32
—— practical philanthropy, 32
—— appeals to British and Foreign Bible Society, 33
Musical instruments for the blind, 35, 38
Music for the blind, 35
—— in mission work, note, 36

NATIONAL Bible Society, Murray joins, 12
—— and the blind, 33-35
—— partial connection continued, 54
Non-Mandarin dialects, note, 9
Numerals, acceptable to Chinese, 7
Numeral Type, how invented, 22
—— explained, 23
—— table for teaching the blind, 25
—— compared with ideograph, 26

OCCUPATION for the blind, 102, 104, 105
Old women respected, 50
Ordination, 52

PEKING syllabary, 408 sounds, 20
—— my visit to, 28
—— Map of, 115
Peter, Blind, 40-43
Postman, work as a, 11
Printing press, note, 91, 95

RAIN, 67-69
Return to Scotland, first, 51
—— second, 107
Ross, the Rev. John, D D., 82, 86, 87
Russell, Professor, pamphlet printed in Peking, 106
—— reprinted, 136-154

SCHOOL for blind men, 33, 62-64
—— women, 53, 59
—— better premises, 111-116
Schools for the blind in five provinces, 119
Shanghai Conference in 1890, 122
Sheng, blind pupil, 27, 32, 43
Shorthand by numbers, 7, 90, 127
—— Invention of, 47, 48
—— Taught by the blind, 48, 49

INDEX

Sighted persons, printing for, 89-106
—— first sighted pupils, 92-96
Square forms acceptable, 7, 101
Stereotyping, 45
—— simple method, 45
—— cards, 49
Stokes on Memory, 12
Superstitions, 54

TELEGRAPHY (domestic, 103), Chinese, 104
Testimony in favour of Mr. Murray's system :—Dr. Ross, 88 ; Dr. Fryer, 108 ; Dr. Stevenson, 123 ; many, 124, 125, 127 ; Dr. Dudgeon, 126; others, 127-132
Tin envelopes for letters, 46

Ting, blind pupil, 32
Tones in Chinese, 20
Tree Kangaroos, 119, 120
Tree of Knowledge, 10

VERSION, one, 99, 100, 117, 126
Versions, one or two, 132
Visible speech, 20
Vision of the Numeral Type, 22

WANG, first blind pupil, 26
—— Two others, 44
Webster, the Rev. James, 77-86
Witchcraft, fear of, 54
Women, blind school for, how commenced, 55. 56
—— earnest blind travellers, 57-59
Writing letters, 45

LONDON:
PRINTED BY GILBERT AND RIVINGTON, LD.,
ST. JOHN'S HOUSE, CLERKENWELL ROAD, E.C.

Miss C. F. GORDON-CUMMING'S
BOOKS OF TRAVEL.

PUBLISHED BY CHATTO AND WINDUS,
111, ST. MARTIN'S LANE, LONDON, W.C

	s.	d.
TWO HAPPY YEARS IN CEYLON. With 28 Illustrations ...	8	6
IN THE HIMALAYAS AND ON INDIAN PLAINS. With 42 Illustrations ...	8	6
IN THE HEBRIDES. With 23 Illustrations...	8	6
VIA CORNWALL TO EGYPT ...	7	6

PUBLISHED BY BLACKWOOD,
45, GEORGE STREET, EDINBURGH.

WANDERINGS IN CHINA ...	10	0
AT HOME IN FIJI ...	7	6
A LADY'S CRUISE IN A FRENCH MAN OF WAR ...	12	0
FIRE FOUNTAINS OF HAWAII. (2 Vols.) ...	25	0
GRANITE CRAGS OF CALIFORNIA	8	6

PUBLISHED BY DOWNEY & CO.,
12, YORK STREET, COVENT GARDEN, LONDON.

THE INVENTOR OF THE NUMERAL TYPE FOR CHINA. One Shilling *nett* ... *Post free*	1	3

www.ingramcontent.com/pod-product-compliance
Lightning Source LLC
Chambersburg PA
CBHW022116160426
43197CB00009B/1049